T0246507

LOVE IS MY FAVORITE FLAVOR

FoodStory

Nina Mukerjee Furstenau, series editor

LOVE IS MY FAVORITE FLAVOR

A MIDWESTERN DINING CRITIC TELLS ALL

Wini Moranville

University of Iowa Press, Iowa City

University of Iowa Press, Iowa City 52242
Copyright © 2024 by Wini Moranville
uipress.uiowa.edu
Printed in the United States of America

ISBN 978-1-60938-961-1 (pbk)
ISBN 978-1-60938-962-8 (ebk)

Design and Typesetting by Ashley Muehlbauer

Printed on acid-free paper

Some brief anecdotes in this book originally appeared
in *dsm magazine* and in *The Bonne Femme Cookbook: Simple,
Splendid Food That French Women Cook Every Day.*

Cataloging-in-Publication data is on file
with the Library of Congress.

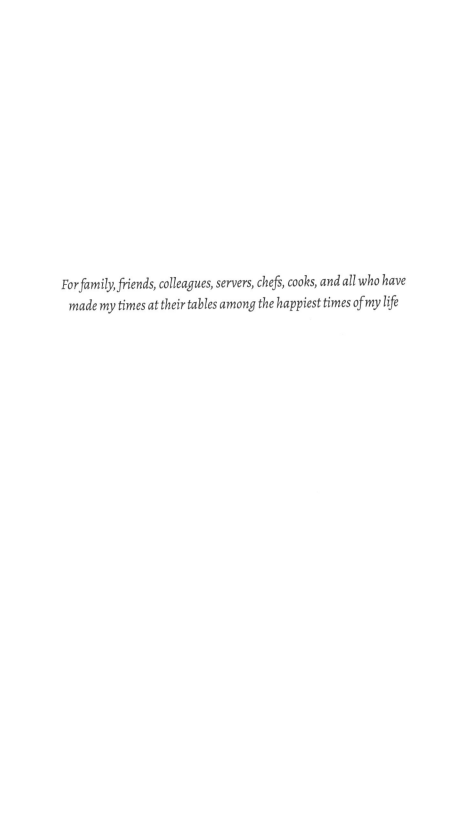

For family, friends, colleagues, servers, chefs, cooks, and all who have made my times at their tables among the happiest times of my life

CONTENTS

PREFACE

The culinary scene has changed much in the twenty-five years since I've been covering it for both local and national publications. And it's changed even more markedly since my early days as a waitress in the kind of once-prevalent restaurants that have long vanished from our landscape: the family-run cafeteria, the department-store tearoom, the street-level downtown coffee shop, one of the last of the hippie-run restaurants.

This book serves as a kind of food and dining history of the past forty-plus years, as seen through the eyes of someone who's experienced it both widely and deeply: working as a server, as a restaurant reviewer in a midsized midwestern city, as a cookbook author, and as a national wine critic going on wine junkets around the world. Over the years, I'm certain we've gained much more than we've lost. But we have lost something. It is through this looking back that we can appreciate just how far American food has come, but also, where our dining culture might be going awry. In doing so, may we reclaim more of what good food, generously shared, does best.

Note that this memoir recounts real experiences I've had throughout my life in food, from serving it to writing about it. I've done my best to tell it like it was; however, out of necessity, I have recreated conversations that I could not possibly remember verbatim. In rare instances I have compressed some events for the sake of narrative flow and envisioned a few minor details to fill in gaps in my memory. Occasionally, I changed the names and identifying characteristics of people who appear here out of respect for their privacy and in hopes that any past foibles and difficulties do not come back to haunt them these many years later.

I WAS THE *DES MOINES REGISTER*'S RESTAURANT REVIEWER. SOMEBODY HAD TO BE.

This chapter's title, of course, echoes the opening sentences of Bill Bryson's book *The Lost Continent*: "I come from Des Moines. Somebody had to." The tone of resignation describes how I sometimes felt on the most challenging days on the job.

Happily though, for about 78 percent of the time, reviewing restaurants was a great gig. Every Thursday morning from 1997 to 2012, my review appeared in the Datebook, the *Des Moines Register*'s weekly entertainment guide; later, I continued to cover Des Moines restaurants for *dsm magazine* many years afterward.

On Thursday mornings, I loved opening my front door, grabbing the physical paper, and seeing how the review looked on the printed page and checking out the photos that ran with it (which I never saw in advance). Thursday was also the day that I always set aside to write and submit my review for the following week.

Back then, reviewing was just one part of how I wove together a living as a food and wine writer. I also wrote for and worked as a project editor on all kinds of magazines and cookbooks, and later websites. While I enjoyed the non-reviewing work—greatly, in fact—it often entailed collaborating with a team of other writers, editors, recipe developers, recipe testers, art directors, graphic designers, photographers, food stylists, prop stylists, and such. Together, we turned out some great cookbooks and magazine food stories, sometimes with moments of discord and tension that creatives often experience when working as a team, but usually with plenty of camaraderie and laughs in between.

But Thursdays were all mine—a nice break from the peopley aspect of everything else I did. I'd bang away on my keyboard in my "free-lancer's hut" (my incredibly unkempt home office) and think about the best way to tell the story of my dining experiences with the goal of doing only one thing: to help readers decide whether the restaurant I was reviewing was worth their hard-earned money and hard-won leisure time.

I never loved the job more than when I was writing about an un-discovered gem that I could bring to light—the review would be a pleasure to write and a boon to both my reader and the restaurateur. Win-win-win. In twenty-plus years of writing about restaurants, the greatest of such moments was in my discovery of Thai Flavors.

One weekday when I was working in the offices of the *Better Homes & Gardens* family of publications, I invited David, a food-magazine editor, to go with me to review a newish hole-in-the-wall joint that was supposed to be good in a greasy spoon kind of way. When we got there, we walked into an empty place, took in the haphazardness of the workspace behind the counter and the dingy furnishings in the dining area, and stood there, waiting for someone to come out of the back room. We might have even called out, "Yoo-hoo! Anyone here?"

But no one came, and frankly, I was a bit relieved. By this time I had a remarkably accurate feel for restaurants that looked bleak at first glance but could be worthy in some other way versus restaurants that were hopeless through and through. I called this sixth sense "mon pif" (my snout), a slang term that a Quebecois friend taught me while we were traveling together in France—he was bemused by my knack for snouting out really good restaurants. As a reviewer, mon pif was generally pretty accurate. I knew this place would never make it, and I had no desire to be the one to nail its coffin shut. We beat a path out of there. The place closed within months, entirely on its own.

I had promised to take David to lunch but was scrambling for an idea of where to go. One of the drawbacks of being a well-known food critic in town is that everyone wants you to decide where to eat. That can be a lot of pressure when you're dining with talented food editors for national publications.

Driving back toward the downtown offices, we spotted a place called Thai Flavors. It was in a scruffy old strip mall, next door to a spay clinic, and yet, mon pif told me something about it looked hopeful. I decided to roll the dice.

We settled into the near-empty, simply furnished space with its tapestry tablecloths under glass and scant Thai decorations here and there. I ordered my go-to Thai dish, a green curry, and David ordered pad Thai. These were hardly the most adventurous dishes on the fifty-plus-item menu, I know, but I wasn't sure if I was truly reviewing the place or just getting a reliable meal to see me through the afternoon.

But then, the most unexpected and amazing thing happened. When the server (a middle-aged man, likely in his fifties) brought David his pad Thai, he set a bowl of soup down in front of me. He did not speak English fluently, but I understood he was telling me, in a friendly but quite matter-of-factly way, that he was bringing me this dish instead of what I ordered. It wasn't a question; it was a statement.

I had a sense that all was going to be just fine. And it was better than fine. The dish had me wide-eyed and reeling, practically giddy with the goofy delight food lovers get when they unexpectedly stumble onto a new and wondrous dish. When it was over, my mood turned more wistful as I said to David, "Why can't all food be this good?"

The dish was tom kha kai—by now a well-known dish in our parts, but new to many local diners at the time. In quintessential Thai fashion, the chicken soup brought a world of great effects into one bowl: the meatiness of chicken and mushrooms; a spicy bite of chiles; a fresh burst of lemongrass; a sweet, smooth, and nutty finish of coconut milk; and a sour touch of lime.

I returned a couple more times on review visits, and the place continued to make me profoundly happy at almost every turn. I also loved the genuine, unrestrained joy of the waitstaff and how they'd do everything they could to steer you right. You could order a dish spiced from one (not very spicy) to five (blowout spicy). On a final review visit, I ventured to order a three. The young server started giggling, and in the sweetest, most amiable way possible, said, "No, no, no! You're a TWO!" I still smile when I think of her. She knew me well.

Des Moines had seen a few Thai restaurants over the years, but this one moved the needle. Accolades practically flew from my fingers as I wrote the review, and after it ran, diners would sometimes have to wait to get a table at lunch. It tickled me to no end to walk in one day and see my four-star review blown up to poster size on the wall of the restaurant. This, my friends, is when reviewing restaurants is truly the best job in the world. No, it's not seeing my words blown up on a wall, but, rather, seeing my words truly connect food lovers with restaurateurs who will bring them joy.

I'm still not sure why the owner brought me the tom kha kai instead of what I ordered, but I think it was in the spirit of one food lover saying to another, "You must try this." Visit after visit—and I continued to go there often over the years—the place was always run by an exuberant waitstaff eager to share their culinary world. In fact, after a while, the owner and staff keyed into my role as a reviewer, and more than once, the owner's father (the guy who had brought me the tom kha kai instead of green curry on my first visit) invited me to go to Thailand and stay with him and his extended family. He said he wanted me to experience Thai food in Thailand. I'm sorry I didn't take him up on it. It surely would have been more meaningful than the rote press junkets I'd go on later in my career.

That first visit to Thai Flavors combined everything wonderful that can happen in a restaurant: great food, yes, but also that marvelous feeling of being in the presence of people who are genuinely glad you're sitting at their table.

Alas, how often did Thai Flavor–like moments happen in the years of reviewing? Not as often as I hoped. It is an honor, a pleasure, and great luck to be a widely read restaurant reviewer, and when it's good, it's one of the best jobs in the world. But you have to get out there and try it all, from the subpar to the sublime.

Bad meals indifferently served come with the territory, and in fact, they weren't even the worst part of the job. No, the hardest part wasn't the rank letdown of a lousy meal. Rather, it was deciding whether or not you're going to tell everyone in town about it, and then actually telling everyone in town about it. Before the days of crowd-sourced reviews (Yelp and the like), I was one of just a handful of voices on the dining scene—and likely the one with the widest circulation. That could be a burden.

And just who was I, anyway, to be such a highly visible voice on the Des Moines dining scene? Had I been a chef? A culinary school grad? Was I even a trained journalist?

In truth, I was none of these; rather, I was simply a longtime waitress turned highly experienced and passionate diner . . . who could write.

LESSONS FROM A LONG-GONE CAFETERIA

My own start in the culinary world was quite humble—so humble, in fact, that at one point just being in a good restaurant where I wasn't the server would have seemed like hitting a jackpot of sorts. Long before I knew there was anything in the universe quite like tom kha kai, I spent about ten years working in the Des Moines restaurant industry. Experiencing firsthand the kinds of joys and struggles that each workday could bring, I began to understand the heart and hard work that lie at the core of running a restaurant. The good, the bad, and the downright weird all served me well in my later years, both as a food and wine writer and as a human being.

Throughout the years I reviewed restaurants, I took immense joy in reporting on great food, of course. Yet I was equally thrilled when I could recount those wonderful moments of care and connection of the sort I enjoyed at Thai Flavors. Such warmth, such generosity—it hovers around love, and even hits the bullseye now and then.

But is it truly reasonable to wish for something like love from a restaurant? Famed twentieth-century chef James Beard, it seems, thought so. Quoted in the *New York Times*, renowned NYC restaurateur Danny Meyer recalled, "James Beard famously told people that when he was stopped in airports and asked what his favorite restaurant was, he answered: 'It's the same as yours. It's the one that loves me the most.'"

The hospitality that Danny Meyer provides in his restaurants is legendary; I've had the great luck to experience it myself at Gramercy Tavern in New York City, where there was unmistakable warmth and expertise to the service, and an uncommonly light touch—no fussing, just that wonderful sense of being in capable, caring hands.

It can be especially life-enhancing when you experience such hospitality in more humble places. It happens. And it always happened, *nearly* without fail, at Baker's Cafeteria.

After I became a restaurant reviewer, the memory of my time spent working there served as a kind of standard for the expert, generous, open-hearted spirit I sought in a restaurant. I often thought back to the way this inexpensive, workaday spot could consistently make everyone—both the customers and the staff—feel cared for and in good hands. I only ever wanted my readers to experience this same level of care.

Growing up, my mother was not my best friend. She was my taskmaster, or at least it felt that way to a tween. Though we did not have day-in, day-out chores to do on our extended family's farm, where we spent large stretches of time, we certainly had them at home in our modest brick house with the yellow door, on the near west side of Des Moines. I had to iron my own clothes by the time I was ten; my sister and I did dishes and cleaned the kitchen after dinner every night. The plates and silverware went into a dishwasher; we hand-scrubbed all pots and pans. But if Mom caught us doing a careless job, she would make us unload the unclean dishes from the dishwasher and wash them by hand as punishment. She did not, by the way, believe in dish-drying racks.

In the summer, my sister, Gretchen, and I each had one room (besides our own) to clean; mine was the bathroom, Gretchen's was the living room. We could do nothing until those rooms were spotless. At the end of one summer, as the school year approached, I mentioned to my mother that she would probably miss having us around to do all her cleaning for her.

She, of course, thought that was pretty darn funny. "Honey," she said, "it's much more work to get you to clean the bathroom—and do it right—than it is for me to clean it myself."

Looking back, of course, I know what she was up to. She instilled in me a work ethic that has served me well all my life. I always felt that the reasons my editors chose me for coveted writing gigs weren't just about talent (there are lots of talented food writers in the world), but also because I always turned things in on time and pretty much ready to publish, with no fuss, drama, excuses, or complaints. Yes, I could write, but I was a workhorse, too, and as such, I made their lives easy, and the assignments kept coming.

Still, at the time I did not know the difference between a mean mom and a good teacher, and I could not wait to get out of the house. The minute I was old enough to work (beyond babysitting), I got an after-school job at Baker's Cafeteria in Des Moines.

I was just shy of fourteen; my sister, three years older than me, had already been working at Baker's for a year or so. My parents were good friends of owners Merle and Junice Baker, who were willing to overlook the requirement that all workers under the age of fourteen obtain a work permit, and my parents didn't mind me working, as the hours were perfect for a kid. You'd get to work at 4:30 and be off by 7:30, an ideal schedule for school nights. I got paid around $2.30 an hour (the going rate for babysitting at the time was seventy-five cents an hour), and I only worked two nights a week plus Sunday afternoons (because . . . school). On those two nights, my sister worked the line while my mother worked the cash register. Not wanting to dine home alone, my dad would often come in and sip coffee and wait for Mom to get a little dinner break so they could eat together.

Baker's was the quintessential midcentury cafeteria. At the beginning of the line, you'd pick up your tray and silverware and a choice of napkins (paper, or—for five cents more—linen). Salads individually plated in little bowls ("monkey dishes," in food-service terms) were embedded in crushed ice, and the selection spun slowly on the salad wheel: spiced apple rings, pickled beets, hard-boiled eggs, iceberg lettuce salad, peach slices, pear halves, cottage cheese with fruit, three-bean salad, kidney-bean salad, and, of course, Jell-O salads, some creamy and fluffy in pastel pinks and light greens, others deeply colored and sparkling like jewels.

Next came the selection of eight or so main dishes. Some were permanent: planks of deep-fried sole, sliced roast beef, and fried chicken. Others rotated in and out regularly: salmon patties and peas, Swiss steak, Salisbury steak, chicken à la king, a very mild spaghetti and meat sauce, and turkey tetrazzini. Many of these dishes appeared unfailingly on given days of the week, and the regular clientele would show up on the nights their favorite dishes were in the rotation. Old-timers especially loved the chicken livers and gizzards served on Sundays.

At the end of the main-dish line were the mashed potatoes with a choice of beef or chicken gravy. The latter was legendary and made from scratch, from pan drippings left over from the equally legendary fried-then-baked chicken.

The bread station offered yeasty homemade dinner rolls, fresh-baked bread sliced from the loaf per order, cornbread, and on Sundays, homemade sweet rolls. A cult favorite of working kids at Baker's was a sweet cinnamon roll slathered with the homemade chicken gravy. The vegetable section was simple: corn, carrots, spinach, green beans, and perhaps one or two rotating specialties, such as Harvard beets, scalloped corn, creamed spinach, or creamed peas and new potatoes.

And then there were the flaky-crust pies, baked fresh each morning, that spun on the pie wheel toward the end of the line: double-crusted fruit pies, like cherry, apple, raisin, blueberry, and raspberry; silky custard pies; meringue-topped pies, like lemon meringue and raisin cream; whipped-cream-topped pies, like banana cream, coconut cream, and chocolate cream.

While any leftover fruit pies may have been held to serve a second day, the cream, custard, and meringue pies were never held past the day in which they were made. At the end of our shifts, we were welcome to sit down and eat whatever slices had not been sold. I can remember eyeing a last piece of raisin cream pie on a rare night—there were hardly ever any pieces left at the end of service—watching it spin around on the wheel and keeping an eye on the clock, thrilled when at 7:30 the "closed" sign in the window was lowered and I could snag that coveted piece.

Baker's opened at 4:30 p.m. for dinner. All the young workers always had dinner together in a cozy and pleasant party-room nook beforehand. We were able to choose pretty much what we wanted (except roast beef), all priced at a 50 percent discount, making that ninety-seven-cent piece of fried sole less than fifty cents, bringing the forty-cent mashed potatoes and chicken gravy down to twenty cents. All drinks were free, so generally, we ate for less than a dollar.

Of course, the teens who worked there thought the food old-fashioned and fuddy-duddy. When a manager told us that we should make our customers feel like Baker's was their home away from home, one smarty-pants boy joked, "More like nursing home away from nursing home."

Still, the time I spent having dinner with the other kids was often a highlight of my day. These days, chefs and restaurateurs make much of the idea of the "family meal"—the chance for the restaurant staff to sit down and eat together. It's a bonding experience, they say, and those who eat well together work well together. But from what I've seen in today's industry, the family meal with everyone sitting down at once is not quite as common in today's restaurants as it once was, at least not on a nightly basis.

At Baker's, it was a key part of the evening. It is true that it made us all know each other better and hence work better together. But it's also how we made friends; it's where we shared gossip and the boys told irreverent jokes. It's where we developed the romantic crushes that made coming to work that much more of a good time.

Looking back, there's also this: you are more likely to get satisfaction in serving your customers good food if you have been served good food yourself. I think the Bakers understood this. They also knew that the kids who worked for them were missing dinner with their families at home (because back then, nearly everyone had dinner with their families at home). And so, they provided us a substitute. They gave us a family meal when such family meals at home were the norm, but well before family meals in restaurants were cool.

The entry-level job at Baker's was carrying trays. After the customer went through the line and received the bill for the meal, a girl would carry their tray to a table for them, then unload the tray, arranging each dish in a precise manner on the table. You had to do this right: place the main plate on the table, the roll of silverware to the right of the plate, the glass of water above the silverware, the cup of coffee or tea to the right of the silverware roll, the pie to the left—and always, always, always make sure the pie pointed toward the diner.

A baby step up from that job was "the cart"—wheeling around a cart of coffee, tea, hot water, and other replenishments diners might need. Boys at the low end of the pecking order either bussed tables or did dishes.

From those low jobs, you could make your way up to a station in the line or kitchen: girls worked on the salad, pie, or vegetable stations of the line; boys worked beverages or helped the chef in the kitchen with short orders or keeping the line replenished. The most senior workers got to work the main-dish line. When you learned to carve roast beef into perfect pink ribbons or quickly and neatly scoop up mashed potatoes, rub a hollow into the mound with the back of the scoop, and ladle just the right amount of gravy into it, all while acting mature enough not to piss off the true adults who also worked the line, well, that was true status at Baker's.

Seniority didn't matter; you had to master each position before you got to move to the next one. If you still acted a bit green at a job, as I did for a while, a more keyed-in girl who started working at Baker's a few months after you might be promoted to vegetables while you were still carrying trays.

What surprises me most, when I look back on it, was how generously staffed this place was. There would be a line of three or four girls standing at the end of the buffet ready to take your tray. Tables were bussed the second the guests left. And then there were the adults, keeping a watchful eye on us all at every turn. Junice and Merle Baker (who were Mr. and Mrs. Baker, to us), and their son, Russ Baker, ran the restaurant, with manager Al Lone and an assistant manager. There were always at least three adults on the floor and an adult cook in the kitchen.

We watched them as they circled the room with a pot of coffee, stopping to touch each table; we saw them step up and bus a table the rare moment when a busboy was busy elsewhere. They carried trays. They talked to guests waiting in the line to help the time pass more quickly. They watched over us, gently correcting us if we placed a slice of pie pointing outward to the void rather than toward the guest. No matter how busy the restaurant got (and we'd sometimes have lines snaking out the front door), the restaurant never became "in the weeds," or too busy to accommodate a special request. I once saw Al Lone walking briskly back to the kitchen from the line to check on something, when a customer stopped him and asked if (a) he had any cheddar cheese he could put on a slice of apple pie, and (b) if he'd heat up the pie with the cheese so that the cheese would melt a bit.

"Sure!" Al said. "Go ahead and get seated and I'll bring it out to you." As if there were nothing to it, as if there weren't about ten kids he had to keep an eye on and thirty people waiting to go through the line, and maybe even possibly a minor issue in the kitchen or dish room he'd been rushing to deal with. We didn't even have a microwave back then—Al had to put the pie in the oven and keep track of the timing in his head while he dealt with everything else, then go out and find wherever it was that guy had been seated. It might have been a hassle for Al, but the vibe at Baker's was such that a customer would never feel sheepish about asking for something they wanted.

The Bakers knew you could never, ever leave any corner of their restaurant in the hands of the fourteen- to sixteen-year-olds. If you did, something like this might happen: one slow summer lunch, I substituted for another teen, and I worked the main-dish line (which I rarely ever got to do). A guy came in and asked for our spaghetti and meat sauce, but the pan of spaghetti on the line was empty. I went to the kitchen window and hollered in an order for a fresh pan of pasta.

"Eighty-six!" the teenage cook hollered back—restaurant lingo for being completely out of an item.

"Sorry," I said to the customer. "We're out of spaghetti noodles. Would you like something else?" He looked over the line, but his gaze kept coming back to the meat sauce. He asked if I could put the red meat sauce over mashed potatoes. Though it sounded gross to me, I did as he requested. He went through the line and sat down at his table.

About three minutes later the cook came out with a pan of spaghetti.

"I thought it was eighty-sixed?" I said.

"No!" he said. "I was only joking! Like we'd ever run out of spaghetti? Duh!"

And that's what happens if you put kids in charge of your restaurant. To this day, I'm mad at that cook, and mad at myself for not having the wherewithal to whip up a plate of spaghetti and meat sauce and bring it out to the guy to replace his off-the-mark combo.

Thankfully, that was an exceedingly rare moment in my two and a half years at Baker's. Their standards were high at every single turn; kids were never in charge. During one of our after-work pie-eating sessions, a boy who had worked in the kitchen complained to our clocked-out group that he had cleaned the short-order grill a little early that night, being as business had been a little slow. And, wouldn't you know, right at 7:30 (which was when we closed), someone came in and ordered a hamburger. He had to fire up the grill, cook the burger, and then reclean the grill.

"That's cold!" I said. "Couldn't you have told him the grill was closed, and he had to order something off the line?"

Al Lone said, curtly and decisively, "Well, you *could* have. But then you would have lost your job." I—along with everyone sitting at that table that night—knew this was no idle threat. You could not say such a thing to a customer and see another day at Baker's.

Their sense of hospitality extended beyond good business. Merle Baker once told my mother that if, from her cashier's stand, she ever saw someone try to walk out without paying, she should just let them go. "They need the food more than I need the money," he said.

And yet, the Bakers were on our side, too. My mother once told me the backstory of one of the girls I worked with. Lila had tried to get a job at another restaurant in town, but they didn't hire her. Her parents suspected it was because of her slightly unique speech patterns.

Rather than have her daughter endure the defeat of applying for another job she wouldn't get, Lila's mother came in and talked to Merle Baker herself, telling him that while her daughter wanted to work, she would not let her daughter go through the heartbreak of applying for a job only to be disqualified again because of the way she spoke.

"I'll give her a job," said Merle Baker. He trained her on the adding machine, the job at the end of the line that required you to tally up the price of the food on each customer's tray—meaning you had to memorize all the prices and work very fast. Lila was a whiz at this. The job also required that you interact with just about everyone. Evidently, Mr. Baker had no intention of hiding this smart, charming girl from his customers, or making her feel unworthy of being a visible part of the operation.

If the Bakers watched us closely as we worked the floor, they watched out for us, too. There was an old man who would come in and sit by himself at the last booth. He was nicely dressed, always in a suit, with wavy white hair and thick glasses, as loveable-looking as somebody's grandfather. He would often try to chat up whatever girl was working the cart, replenishing coffee cups. One night, as I started to walk away from a lengthy chat with him, he reached out his hand, as if wishing to shake it as a goodbye or thank-you gesture. Then, he grasped my hand and held it for about three seconds longer than I felt he should have.

That's when eagle-eyed Russ Baker came by and said, "Hey, Wini. Back to work." He steered me into the back room and said, "Keep clear of that guy. I'll refill his coffee cup from now on."

It was obvious that Russ didn't like the customer touching my hand, and I was pretty sure I understood why. Perhaps the guy was, as Russ surmised, a bit perverse. But then in the blink of an eye, the years passed. I was into my forties, dining in a restaurant, when a young waitress's hand bumped into mine as she was clearing something from my table. Inadvertently and unmistakably, I felt the plumpness and smoothness of her soft, youthful hand against my bonier older one, and suddenly, that long-forgotten moment at Baker's came back to me, and I got a sense of what that guy might truly have been reaching for.

There are many places in the world where the wonder of living reveals itself, but in my life, the greatest of these have always been at the table.

Oh, yes, and I loved the money, too. I can still remember the thrill of getting my first paycheck. That $2.30 hourly wage in 1974 was equivalent to nearly $15 today. My friends Cindy and Kirsten, who worked as maids at a motel up the street, met me at Baker's after they got off their shift, drinking Cokes at a table until it was time for me to clock out. The Baker's cashier let me cash the check at the restaurant; I had more money in one place than I'd ever had in my life, and together, Cindy, Kirsten, and I went to the Kmart across the street, where I spent almost every dime of it. I bought a Led Zeppelin album, way too much low-budget makeup, and a pair of cheap dangly earrings.

As an impulse buy in the checkout aisle, I bought an insanely huge bag of cashews (ninety-seven cents—I can still see the big round red sticker on the cellophane bag). Cashews were a rare treat in our house, where less expensive peanuts were the nut of choice. We polished off the bag as we sat on a bench outside Kmart waiting for one of our moms to pick us up. They were so good and so plentiful.

Danny Meyer is often quoted on the art of hospitality; this is one of my favorites of his many gems on the subject: "Hospitality is almost impossible to teach. It's all about hiring the right people."

Where do these "right people" come from? Perhaps there is a kind of hospitality gene; indeed, in all my years of reviewing, now and then I sensed that some people had it, others didn't. But nurture must come into it, too. I was lucky that my family's farm and my family table played such key roles in my early life. I was also lucky that my very first job was at Baker's Cafeteria. I honestly think that Meyer would have been fortunate to hire just about anyone who had spent a stretch of their youth working in this humble but much-loved spot, where hospitality wasn't so much taught but rather became part of the air we breathed.

JUST DOWN THE ROAD, THERE'S
A PLACE LIKE . . .

By the time I was sixteen, I had worked more than two years at Baker's
Cafeteria. That changed when, the summer after my sophomore year
in high school, my friends Cindy and Kirsten started working at a local
Country Kitchen. A twenty-four-hour casual restaurant franchise
with a few relatively new outposts in town, they had this annoying
jingle on the radio:

> *Just down the road, there's a place like home . . . Country Kitchen . . .*
> *Where wearin' a smile is right in style . . . Country Kitchen . . .*

Cindy and Kirsten's hours were longer and less school-kid friendly
than mine at Baker's. While I worked from 4:30 to 7:30, they had to
work from 4:30 to 9:00. But the difference was this: when they got off
work, they had a pocket full of change—and that change added up.
They worked for tips and made twice per hour what I was making. For
a teenager—at least for one like me, whose basic needs were met by
their parents—that brought the potential for a lot of cheap makeup,
dangly earrings, record albums, and cashews.

And so I handed in my notice at Baker's. I put my deposit down on
the required light-brown uniform with its contrasting dark-brown
apron and the annoyingly uncool brown-and-white checkered bandana,
I polished up my white work shoes I had bought for Baker's, and I
went to work serving Country Boy and Country Gal combos (burgers
or sandwiches with fries and coleslaw), breaded chicken likely pulled
from the freezer and thrown in the fryer, low-grade steaks that came
frozen in a box, chef's salads with planks of yellow and white cheese

and processed meats, Reubens with corned beef that looked more like bologna, and other stripes of mediocre chain food.

Even at that early age, I knew there was a lot of difference between the mostly house-made food they served at Baker's and the stuff they served at Country Kitchen. The first time I sampled one of their food-truck-purveyed apple pies, with its goopy filling of uniform tidbits of mushy apples in a weirdly soft, oddly bitter crust, I wondered if anyone would willingly eat such a thing, much less pay to do so. But diners seemed to put up with it—the pie was served microwave-hot with cinnamon ice cream. When I worked there, Baker's didn't even own a microwave; at Country Kitchen, I learned that many people liked hot, mediocre pie just as well as they did room-temperature homemade pie—especially if it was served with cinnamon ice cream and cost a few cents cheaper a slice.

I soon found that working for tips made the night go so much faster, as there was always a bit of anticipation and excitement to see what, if anything, would be left on the table for me. Back then, in my experience, only about half of the population tipped, and usually, it was just a few coins (rarely even 10 percent). Still, it was thrilling, walking out of work with the uniform weighed down by a pocket full of change. I always had cash, and because I also got a paycheck every two weeks to go into the bank for savings, the jangle of change always felt like mad money.

Finally, after years of wearing hand-me-downs from my older sister, or clothes my mother had made (the memory of which I cherish now, but back then, I wasn't a fan), I was able to buy clothes I loved. I could wear them immediately off the rack instead of enduring that long wait (probably a few days, but an eternity to a kid) between when I picked out patterns and cloth at a fabric store and when Mom finally completed the project at her sewing table in the basement.

And yet, the extra money came at a price—something known in the restaurant industry as "sidework." For the privilege of working a shift and making tips, after your section was closed, you had to spend another hour—in which you were not earning tips—doing the work of keeping the restaurant clean. The tasks you were assigned depended on the section you worked that night. For instance, the Section A servers, in addition to dusting, vacuuming, and replenishing the salt, pepper, and sugar in their own sections, might have had to tidy the bathrooms. For Section B, the extra job could be to clean and replenish the ice cream freezer and refill all the more-than-half-empty ketchup bottles in the restaurant (a gross job that required pouring the contents of nearly empty bottles into a plastic funnel, refilling the half-empty bottles with the ketchup from the funnel, then wiping the tops of the crusty bottles "clean" with a rag). Section C might have to do something like straighten up the break room, sweeping up and emptying all the dirty ashtrays and clearing away sticky soda glasses that had sat all day—some with cigarettes butts in them when the ashtrays overflowed. God only knows what Section D had to do, but all of it was much grubbier work than I had ever done at Baker's, because at Country Kitchen, in addition to being servers, we were, basically, sixteen-year-old janitors.

On weekends, after leaving work at Baker's, I could generally go directly to whatever the rest of the evening held for me—movies or basketball games, or hanging out in the basements of friends. In the ladies' room, I'd slip out of my white uniform and into my hand-me-downs and be on my way. After a shift at Country Kitchen, however, I felt grimy; after five hours of wearing a bandana, my hair would be flattened into a style we called "bandana head." I'd have to go home and scrub myself clean and completely rework my hair. But at least I slipped into store-bought clothes that were all mine.

The management style was different at Country Kitchen as well. The Bakers made it clear that school always came first: if you had a schedule conflict due to something school related, the Bakers would always work around it. Kids who went to church were allowed to clock in later (yet had to leave later) on Sundays than those who didn't. You could always have Wednesdays off if you attended Wednesday after-school church programs.

At Country Kitchen, *sometimes* they'd work around your school schedule, but generally, they wouldn't. If you couldn't work a particular night you were scheduled, you had to find someone to replace you.

With very few exceptions, the Bakers would never let a slew of teenage workers loose on the floor without supervision, but that's exactly what happened at Country Kitchen. Sometimes, the manager on duty would disappear into his little windowless office for much of the shift. On the busiest evenings, the place could descend into bedlam, and you'd be left to fend for yourself: arguing with the cooks over incomplete orders, dealing with annoyed patrons whom the indifferent hostess had seated at sticky tables that you hadn't yet had a chance to wipe down, going into the dish room and washing silverware by hand when the dishwashers decided to disappear for a smoke during the middle of a rush.

When things broke down, the management's attitude seemed to be, "If you want to make your tips, you'll figure it out."

No wonder sometimes when Cindy, Kirsten, and I would drive to work together, we'd sing, "Just down the road, there's a place like hell. . . ."

Serving mediocre-to-bad food also wore on me. Most of the time, people were satisfied enough; the breakfast dishes and burgers were the most popular items, and they were fine. But I was heartbroken when people at my tables weren't happy with what they ordered. I can still recall the disappointed face of a young man dining alone as he ate one of our low-grade steaks (likely a splurge for him). He left much of the dry, gristly thing on the plate. As I cleared his dishes, I told him it didn't look like he enjoyed it so much. He said, mustering a smile as if I were the one to be consoled, "That's okay. Next time I'll just order something else."

I could hardly bear that he took such a letdown so easily, as if it happened daily. And it pained me even more that I had been the conduit to his lousy meal. We had not held up our end of the bargain, and I was the face of his disappointment.

While I never once saw anyone steal anything from Baker's, at Country Kitchen, management sometimes complained that the cash register came up short. I remember seeing someone on staff steal steaks by hiding them under their coat as they walked out the door after their shift. I saw servers load up the tables of their friends with food, then charge them only for the price of a few Cokes. Even I didn't think twice about putting a couple of individually portioned hot-fudge packets into my apron before I walked out the door.

I also got a taste of the bitterness that could emerge among servers in low-end restaurants of the time. Hollywood would have you believe that such servers are either upbeat, wisecracking sages or else simply sad and kindhearted (à la Michelle Pfeiffer in *Frankie and Johnny*). While such clichés had some basis in some of the older servers I encountered, a few others I worked with both at Country Kitchen and elsewhere went through their days with a petty meanness that came with either mounting years of disappointments or a sense that this would be their life.

Once, when a new female manager was hired, I thought the other waitresses I worked with would be pleased that for once we had a woman as a manager, rather than the usual slew of almost-middle-aged men. But the consensus among a few other waitresses was that the new manager had attained her achievement "lying flat on her back all the way."

One slow night at Country Kitchen, I went back to the break room to tell a server named Patty that some customers in her section had been waiting a while to get their check. I thought I was being helpful —perhaps saving her from being stiffed (industry speak for losing a tip). Instead of thanking me, she stamped out her cigarette and, as she walked past me, blew smoke in my face. The other workers in the break room laughed.

I learned quickly to stick to my tribe—Cindy, Kirsten, and others I'd grown friendly with—and avoid as much as I could those who seemed beaten down by the biz. Even then, I could understand why they were bitter, but that didn't mean I liked being an easy target for their resentment.

And yet, for all its downsides, working at Country Kitchen had its moments. It was the mid-1970s: Fleetwood Mac played from the mini jukeboxes at each booth almost all the time, and when it didn't, I'd plug in some quarters from my pocket full of tips to hear some more. Bussing tables and doing sidework to "Over My Head"—while feeling a bit over my head about someone myself—beat carrying trays to Baker's fuddy-duddy Muzak tapes of "Satin Doll" any day.

Getting into a groove and keeping ahead of it all during our busiest times while scooping loose change from the tables into my apron pockets was a blast. And, for the most part, I liked the clientele. Taking care of a party from the moment they sat down until they left was so different than merely carrying someone's tray at Baker's. I got to know them a bit. It was here that I first discovered that I enjoyed making people happy at the table. I sometimes wonder if my stretch at Country Kitchen was a harbinger to my later work as a restaurant reviewer. I tried to steer diners toward something they'd enjoy, and it pleased me immensely when they did but crushed me hard when they didn't.

I still remember a little blonde boy ordering pecan pie for dessert, but he didn't know how to pronounce it. He said, "I'll have the peek-in pie." The older men at the table laughed meanly at him, and later when I set the slice down, they razzed him: "Oh look, there's your peek-in pie, Davey!" "Yeah, you'd better peek in and see what's there." Hardy-har-har.

I wanted to think this was all some kind of good-natured ribbing, but then I saw the boy's lack of delight as he slowly ate the pie, the way his mother put her arm around him as if trying to comfort him. That pie should have been one the sweetest parts of his day, but it wasn't.

On rare but splendid occasions, later in the evening boys we liked from school came in and sat in our sections to tease and cajole Cindy, Kirsten, and me while we finished up our sidework. Those were the best nights of all.

I had joined the high school marching band, playing cymbals (it was the only thing I could play; besides it allowed me to hang out with cute drummers), and I had been unable to get someone to cover my shift on a key game night one Saturday. A few days earlier, when I went in to plead with a manager to let me have the evening off, he refused, telling me I'd have to quit before that night if I couldn't get someone to work for me. To make sure I knew who was boss, he told me that effective immediately he was also planning to extend my hours from 9:00 p.m. on weekends to 10:00 p.m.—something my parents patently forbade. I had been pushing it with the 9:00 p.m. time, they said.

That Saturday, I came in and told the manager that I would have to quit, since I could not work that night and had found no one to cover my shift. I handed in my uniform, for which the restaurant was to refund my deposit. I went into the break room to say goodbye to the few people who cared. When I saw the schedule grid posted by the time clock, with my name and all the nights I was to work the next week, I took out a pen and scratched a line through my name. I didn't want people to think that I simply wasn't showing up for my shifts. Or maybe I was, as the manager later deduced, being a little snotty.

As I walked out the back door, he caught me and admonished me for touching his schedule. "I'm the only one who gets to write on the schedule board," he bellowed. "That is *not your property*."

He handed back my uniform and told me the restaurant would not reimburse me for it. The reason? He was just sticking it to me.

The following Monday night, my father drove me back to the restaurant. I sat in the car while he went inside with my uniform to see the manager. I have no idea what my father said to him, but when Dad got back into the car, he handed me the money for my uniform in cash.

"Hash-slinging is no business to be in," he said.

A PLUM GIG

Sometimes you don't get where you want to go very quickly. And sometimes, you have no idea how a downbeat, dead-end job could possibly serve you deeply and meaningfully years later. As is the case with most people who take a long time to groove into a gig they love, it was a jagged path getting there.

I worked in quite a few Des Moines restaurants while in high school, on breaks in college, and for a dispiriting stretch after college into my midtwenties. When I finally realized no one in town (outside of retail and restaurants) was going to hire someone with a BA in French and English, I hightailed it to New York City to try my luck there. After a decent job in French banking and a laughably bad job at a glamorous women's magazine, I finally found my footing in the book publishing industry, where I gained the kind of editorial experience that would later help me finally hit my stride.

By 1997, I had returned to Des Moines and had been working as a freelance food writer and editor, mostly for books and magazines within the Meredith/*Better Homes & Gardens* family of publications. Word got out that the *Des Moines Register* needed a new Datebook Diner, the paper's restaurant reviewer, to replace the recently departed one; someone at Meredith (a few blocks away from the *Register*) kindly put forth my name. I applied, wrote two tryout columns, and snagged the job.

The freelance position sounded like a plum gig. And yet, less than thirty minutes into dinner on the very first night I visited a restaurant for my very first review, I learned it would be a little dicier than it sounded.

Not only was I responsible for writing the dining column, but it was also entirely up to me to choose which restaurants to review. While editors might suggest places they had heard of, no one gave me a "must-do" list or nudged me toward certain places. The only stipulation was that any restaurant I reviewed could not have been reviewed within the last two years unless significant changes had taken place—which rarely happened in the static restaurants of the time.

It's hard to believe my naivete, but when I took on the gig, I honestly envisioned only writing about restaurants I loved or at least liked. Who wants to be a meanie? Plus, I had absolutely no desire to write about mediocre or bad meals—that would require me to actually eat mediocre and bad meals, and who in their right mind wants to do that? I would seek out what was great and ignore the rest.

So, for my first review in September 1997, I headed to a neighborhood bar and grill I'd been to dozens of times since I returned to Des Moines in 1991. It was a cozy spot that had a thriving bar scene but a gem of a little restaurant as well: top-notch sandwiches and steaks and a handful of pasta dishes, along with a few nightly specials that showed the kitchen could do more than sandwiches and steaks and pasta.

And yet, the experience was a train wreck of the first degree. I don't remember exactly why the food was so lackluster that night, but it was way off its mark. I started wondering how I would eloquently word a piece to say something like, "Hey, normally this place is really great, but the first night I went in to review it, it kind of sucked."

But then things got really weird.

A couple seated across from us had ordered some sort of fish dish that they found less than acceptable. They flagged the server, who apologized and said she'd ask the owner to stop by the table.

The owner came out and was initially reasonable and polite, saying he'd be glad to substitute something else or simply take the meal off the tab. That was positive; I knew from experience that misfires happen in restaurants all the time. It's how the staff deals with them that makes or breaks the experience.

But then, for no reason that has ever made any sense to me, the owner grabbed a fork from another table and tasted the fish straight from the plate on the table in front of the customer. And not just one taste. He actually stood there and started eating the guy's fish, bite after bite, saying something like, "Actually, I think this is pretty good. . . . I'm surprised you didn't like it." He kept eating the fish and talking about it and *would not leave the couple alone*. I began to wonder if he weren't a bit stewed.

Such moments became what I would come to call "Datebook Diner moments," and they occurred every so often when I went in to review a place. I'd be sitting in a restaurant, halfway through a meal, and I'd say to my dining companion (usually my husband, Dave), "There's no way I'm going to review his place."

Because when it comes to restaurant reviewing, the only thing worse than enduring a really bad meal is having to go home and re-live the whole fiasco through writing about it. There's no joy in that whatsoever.

A review had to be based on at least four meals ordered. You could order two meals for two people across two visits or four meals for four people on one visit. I usually went twice (with myself and another diner), as it gave me a chance to really think about the restaurant's strengths and flaws, then go back and see if my initial findings remained on the mark.

The *Register* had a scrupulous policy that if the critic was going to give less than a two-and-a-half-star rating (out of five stars), then the critic had to visit the restaurant again to give the restaurant one more chance to redeem itself.

In theory, it was a good policy—it meant we were trying to give a restaurant a fair shake. But in practice, it meant I was usually destined to eat yet another really bad meal. That would entail up to three rotten turns at the table. And for what? To write a review that would make absolutely no one happy? The restaurant's business could suffer (with the ripple effect that servers might be out some income via reduced tips), and my readers would be none the wiser when it came to finding a great meal they'd love. I'd lie awake in bed at night freaking out about every single word I'd written—the journalist's ethic of being scrupulously fair and accurate felt even more onerous when I was dealing with people's livelihoods.

So, for my first review, I scratched the weird experience and headed to Skip's, another neighborhood restaurant that was always a sure thing. Fortunately, they came through for me, and I was able to truthfully write a positive review, commending the place for the way it took "the best of Iowa steakhouse traditions, and moved on from there."

I spent the next couple weeks following pretty much the same drill. I tried my best to find places that I could mostly praise, but it was harder than it sounded. The Datebook Diners before me had already snagged the very best places in town—the shoo-ins I wanted to write about fell within that two-year "do not review yet" window. There simply weren't one-hundred-plus great, newsworthy restaurants in town in 1997.

On my fourth review, I thought I was in for a sure thing. However, a steakhouse/red-sauce pasta spot that had been around for over two decades—one that I had appreciated in the distant past—simply did not hold up. The steaks tasted like low-grade chain-restaurant cheapies, and the atmosphere reminded me of a "Mr. Steak with the lights dimmed." The service, however, was expert and welcoming.

The easiest thing in the world would have been for me to overlook the low-quality meat and give the venue a thumbs-up review with a few read-between-the-lines caveats. Focus on the warm service, talk about how the thin fried onion rings passed my own test for the best of their kind—that is, they flaked all over my shirt when I ate them. Go on and on about icy-cold gimlets served straight up, with little shards of ice elegantly swirling around the glass.

Certainly, I did applaud what was good. But I had to tell about the rest, too.

From the first review I wrote, I knew that for me, the reader's trust was everything. Akin to my days waiting tables, I felt it was my duty to lead people to meals they'd enjoy and to help them avoid meals they wouldn't. If, after more than two decades, I still felt the weight of serving that young man a gristly steak at Country Kitchen, I now felt the pressure to not mislead tens of thousands of readers. If I repeatedly praised mediocre restaurants and gave cagey thumbs-ups to downright dreadful places, why should readers believe me when I uncovered a true gem?

I was running out of time and resources. While I had thought it would be easy enough to just ignore a bad restaurant and move on to a better one to write about, I soon found out why that strategy wasn't going to work. The *Register* gave me a finite expense account. It was up to me to find four restaurants worth writing about with a three-hundred-and-twenty-dollar monthly budget. If I reviewed a budget-buster like 801 Chophouse one week, I'd end up reviewing delis and tearooms and pizzerias for the next few weeks. The costs had to average out to eighty dollars a week.

I had no extra budget for misfires. If I didn't end up reviewing a restaurant I visited, I would have to pay for it out of my own pocket. At first, I didn't mind, but soon it became pricey to cut and run.

Fortunately, my expense allowance improved somewhat as the years went by. Nevertheless, throughout my fifteen-year tenure, I often ended up supplementing my reviewing with my own money. It helped that my work as a freelance food writer and editor was lucrative enough to allow me to do so. Meredith, in a way, was unwittingly supplementing the *Register*'s food coverage.

The upside of the *Register*'s less-than-opulent budget was that it helped keep me honest. It's one thing to dine out on someone else's dime and find it mostly fine(ish), but how did I really feel about a place when I was reaching into my own pockets to pay for it, like everyone else?

The two-and-half-star review ran, and I held my breath, waiting for the restaurant to close, or at least for the restaurateur and his staff and loyal customers to ride me out of town on a rail.

Nothing of the sort happened, of course. Indeed, knowing what I later learned, I'm sure that the place was just as busy—if not even busier—in the days and weeks after my review ran.

When I mentioned my distress about giving less-than-thumbs-up reviews, my editor told me the story of a fine Mexican restaurant that had been pretty much trashed by a previous reviewer. A few years earlier, when it had first opened, the venue had truly rolled the dice, serving a kind of upscale Mexican food that most Des Moines diners were not yet ready to embrace. I personally remember loving their amazing duck tacos.

By the time the last critic had gone in to review the place, the restaurant had—likely in a last-ditch attempt to stay afloat—added a selection of Mexican food more in line with local expectations: giant burritos, cheesy enchiladas, gooey chiles rellenos, and the like, all served with rice, beans, chips, and salsa. While these new items were less head-turning, they were cheap and abundant. The critic didn't like this transition at all, and she said so in very clear terms.

And yet, when my editor happened to drive by the place the night after the review ran, the parking lot was jam-packed. The review had given the restaurant visibility in that "no publicity is bad publicity" kind of way. But it had also keyed readers into the fact that the place was no longer solely focused on high-end, highly detailed food. Now, the food was cheap and abundant.

The steakhouse I reviewed would hum along just fine, because more than once in the piece I described the refreshingly low cost of dining at this restaurant. I wrote that the food was a "bargain," and a "good value." Putting a finer point on it, I wrote: "If you're looking for lots of food at a good price, [this restaurant] is a reasonable option."

That, it seemed, was the magic formula. In those days, many, many readers seemed to be quite happy with so-so food—as long as it was cheap and abundant. And if the service was top-notch (which it was), all the better.

In 1997, there were still plenty of diners around who had lived through the Great Depression and others who had raised families during the inflationary 1970s and the high-unemployment 1980s. Even in good times, the habits of those who have been frugal out of necessity die hard. And even when the economy is booming, plenty of people value quantity (at a cheap price) over quality at a higher price, especially if it gets you out and into a bustling dining room to see and be seen.

You have no idea how happy I was to find that all I had to do to avoid feeling *too* bad about writing a less-than-glowing review was to somehow intimate that the food was inexpensive and the portions were generous. Such a review might hurt a restaurateur's feelings, but as long as I mentioned the inexpensive and generous portions, I probably wouldn't hurt the venue's business. In fact, the publicity—with those magic words—could even help.

By the way, that steakhouse is still going strong, celebrating more than fifty years of serving pretty much the same style of inexpensive midwestern steakhouse food and continuing to make many, many diners very, very happy.

DINING AT THE COOLEST
RESTAURANT IN TOWN, 1997

When I first started reviewing restaurants, I worried that my far-flung dining experiences might not serve me so well. In the 1980s, I had lived in New York City, where I'd experienced a world of great food. By the 1990s, I'd begun spending long stretches of each summer in France. While I'd always admired what Des Moines restaurants did best—such as a great steak, flaky onion rings, and an icy-cold gimlet—I also knew there could be more to a city's dining life than what it already had.

The full parking lots and long wait lists at mediocre restaurants such as that steakhouse I had reviewed early on led me to believe that Des Moines diners were mostly happy with the way things were. Did anyone really want me to point out that they could be better? Des Moines hates a snob; the city could not care less how things are done in New York, much less the south of France. For about a year, I struggled between cagily going along with the status quo and saying what I really thought.

Thankfully, a few weeks into my tenure, a visionary restaurant named Bistro 43 opened its doors in a charming little spot—a former Maid-Rite restaurant—in a quaint old Des Moines neighborhood. The venue was owned by the chef/pastry-chef team of Jeremy and Kristin Morrow (who were married at the time), and a third partner, Robert Fisher, who ran the front of the house. Actually, front of the house is a bit of a misnomer, being that there was no front and back; rather, the restaurant's ten tables lined one side of the room, with an open kitchen lining the other.

Blown away by their ambition, and the fact that they pulled it off with aplomb, I awarded the place five stars. Then I held my breath to see if Des Moines would catch on.

The restaurant indeed took off. In response to high demand for reservations, they soon expanded from the ten-table spot, opening up more seating in a former laundromat next door while still keeping the high standards intact. After watching this place thrive, I knew there were some Des Moines diners who were hungry—and willing to pay—for something more than what they'd always had. Witnessing Bistro 43's success helped me find my voice and raise my standards as a reviewer.

The food was terrific—I still remember a pan-roasted, locally raised heirloom-breed pork chop with smoked cheddar grits and a sprightly pear-jicama salad. I recall, above all, that the dish *sparkled*—it glistened thanks to the freshness of the ingredients, the immediacy of being whisked from an open kitchen just a few steps away, and the risk-taking imagination of the chef and staff. I thought, *This is what pork smelled and tasted like on my uncles' Iowa farm—truly porky—before it was bred to be so lean.* With this dish and others that were equally original and energetic and honest, Des Moines began to awaken from its steakhouse/spaghetti-joint slumber. We would always have the former kinds of restaurants, but soon there were options.

I loved the way the Tennessee-born chef brought a few signature southern twists to his food: grits, fried green tomatoes, barbecued-ham egg rolls. He helped introduce Iowa to the idea of "chef-driven" food—one-of-a-kind dishes that veered well off the beaten path from the shrimp scampi, steak Diane, and sole amandine that often graced fine-dining menus at the time.

Yet the Morrows were also attuned to a sense of place. Bistro 43 was the first restaurant I'd been to in the city where the names of local farmers and producers starred on the menu. It was also one of the first local menus I encountered that truly changed with the seasons; in fact, you can probably guess that I reviewed the restaurant in autumn by my descriptions of the pear-jicama garnish on the chop and the thoroughly seasonal dessert I was served: apple flan with a pool of apple-cider-infused caramel glaze. With that dish, pastry chef Kristin Morrow raised the bar for desserts in our town.

Visionary chefs in California started the fresh-local-seasonal movement sometime in the 1970s, but it would take a couple more decades for the ethos to be as sure-footed elsewhere; in fact, it would have been rare to find something like jicama or pears on an heirloom pork chop even in 1980s New York. In 1997, for a chef to make this kind of culinary vision thrive in Des Moines took grit, imagination, hard work—and a wing and a prayer.

Other restaurants in town had tried, but this one had staying power. The restaurant lasted for six years (a good run for small, chef-driven bistros in Des Moines). Even after the restaurant closed, the chef continued to share his vision and talents in two spin-off restaurants, a small French-inspired bistro and a grander fine-dining spot in the historic Hotel Fort Des Moines. He later worked at an ambitious fine-dining downtown restaurant at the Kirkwood, another historic hotel building. He also helped usher in a more polished style of bar-grill dining at Star Bar, where you can still enjoy a take on his barbecue chicken spring rolls, even if he himself has long left the field to become an educator. We were lucky to have him the years we did.

While the food was terrific, and the ambiance was perfect for the energetic vibe, the service truly helped distinguish the place. In the first paragraph of my review, I wrote:

As we walked up the stairs to the humble entrance to Bistro 43, the waiter caught our eye through the window, dashed to open the door, and warmly welcomed us into the bustling dining room. From that moment on, every little thing the staff did was wrought with expertise and graciousness.

On this and subsequent visits, Bistro 43 had a knack for making you feel truly welcome the minute you walked through the door—it was as if it was *you* they'd been waiting to see all night. I loved the way the servers described the food with enthusiasm, but without sounding like know-it-alls.

There was a camaraderie, a connection, among the servers and the diners. They weren't overly familiar, but they were unmistakably genuine. I remember bumping into two of the servers in the frozen food aisle of the local supermarket. They smiled when they saw me, saying something like, "Yes, here we are, buying frozen entrées on our night off!"

I showed them the frozen pizza in my basket, and we all cracked up.

That was the spirit of the place. Great food, expert service, but something else, too. Joy? Connectedness? Yes—and a wholehearted effort to avoid pretentiousness at all costs. It all combined into a hard-to-define quality I could always feel but rarely describe.

That's not to say everything was great every single visit. By about the third or fourth time I dined at Bistro 43 (for my own enjoyment, well after the review ran), the staff had keyed into the fact that I was the *Register*'s food critic. A former student of my husband's, who knew I wrote the *Register*'s reviews, had begun working in the open kitchen —she blew my cover.

Instead of making the service better (frankly, it could not have been better), being recognized added awkwardness to the experience. While still congenial, the waiters became overly attentive, perhaps asking too many times what I thought of each dish, filling my water glass after I'd taken just one sip. The fussing diminished that perfect balance of expertise and easygoingness that I had loved.

Of course, what they were doing came from the right place, and that made all the difference.

Amid my admiration for the servers at Bistro 43, I also sometimes felt a wince of regret. Here they were, working at the coolest restaurant in town, yet making you feel you were in the in-crowd, too. It's a gift to be able to do so—a gift I simply did not have when, in high school, I worked at a 1977 equivalent of Bistro 43. While the Soup Kitchen wasn't by any means a gourmet restaurant, it was among the coolest places in town to dine. I only wish I had consistently offered the same kind of openheartedness back then as the servers at Bistro 43 did in 1997.

WORKING AT THE COOLEST
RESTAURANT IN TOWN, 1977

In 1977, the area around Drake University in Des Moines swelled with all kinds of thriving offbeat venues. The creaky old buildings—originally home to businesses like hardware stores, meat markets, bakeries, shoe repair shops, and newsstands—now buzzed with record shops, head shops, natural food stores, a greasy spoon or two, and quirky bars and restaurants with names like Beggar's Banquet, Mustard's Last Stand, So's Your Mother, and the Blind Munchies.

The grooviest of them all was the Soup Kitchen.

This vegetarian restaurant was housed in a long, narrow two-story old brick storefront with apartments on the top floor; the building looked like it had once been a mom-and-pop grocery. Inside, it still had the original wooden floors and stamped-tin ceilings. The owners, Glen and Grace, had hung leafy plants from macramé hangers in the windows; they furnished the dining room with mismatched wooden chairs and tables, a bright-orange upright piano, and a jungle mural painted floor to ceiling along one long side wall by artist Mindy Miller, the daughter of the *Des Moines Register*'s Pulitzer Prize–winning editorial cartoonist, Frank Miller.

The walls in the restrooms were lined top to bottom with shellacked clippings from late-1960s and mid-1970s magazines, with everything from scantily clad *Playboy* hotties to political cartoons and iconic photographs—Kent State, the children running from a napalm attack in Vietnam, Nixon waving his absurd victory signs as he boarded the helicopter to leave the White House forever.

My high school gang (mostly band nerds) considered ourselves part of something infinitely more cutting edge than marching band when, after playing at football games, we stopped going to the local deep-dish pizza place and started hanging out at the Soup Kitchen for whole-wheat pizza crust topped not only with classics like mushrooms, green onions, and olives but also with corn, peas, celery, sprouts, and just about anything that wasn't meat. Waiting for our orders, we'd drink sweet organic pineapple-coconut juice or Roastaroma tea while reading well-worn old copies of the *Village Voice* that were always lying around.

One school day, my friends Gretel and Joe and I all headed to the Soup Kitchen for lunch. While we waited for cream cheese and broccoli sandwiches and carob brownies, Joe sat down at the orange piano and played the moving and melodic piano exit to "Layla."

I had known Joe since seventh grade; to me, he was always a bit of a gawky, short, skinny kid whose eyeglasses were continually smudged. But by eleventh grade, he had grown tall and had become cool in a *Twelve Dreams of Dr. Sardonicus*–listening, Kurt Vonnegut–reading kind of way. He was also, up until that time, the most talented musician I had ever met. He could play anything by ear on the piano.

And that day, he was playing the most tortured and romantic song of the '70s on the orange piano at the Soup Kitchen.

When our order was ready, the woman at the shellacked-wood counter told us the musician's meal was free. It was touching, especially since Joe had really entertained no one but us; the only people in the restaurant at the time were the three of us and this extremely compelling young woman at the counter.

As we ate our sandwiches and brownies, I watched as the heavily pregnant, dark-haired woman wiped down tables and set up for the dinner rush. Years later, my good friend Ann, a film critic, would describe a young actress as having a "peaches-and-organic-yogurt complexion," and the minute I read those words, I thought back to Grace. I quickly attributed her striking natural beauty and luminous glow to the wholesome food she served and ate. I soon became a vegetarian and remained so for one year.

Gretel and I went to the Soup Kitchen so often that everyone who worked there knew us well. One warm autumn night, we headed there without Joe for pizza. We parked in the back, and as we walked by an open kitchen window along the side of the building, a guy yelled through the screen at us, "Hey you two! Get in here and get these dishes done!"

Though he was kind of, sort of kidding, Gretel and I immediately went in through the back door. There was Glen, Grace's husband and the co-owner, standing in the back amid a slew of dirty dishes stacked in bus tubs while he was trying to keep up with the pizza orders tacked on a corkboard strip on the wall.

"Sure!" I said. I had heard of people washing dishes for their suppers, and now, there we were.

He quickly showed us how to operate the tiny round automatic dishwasher and then went back to making pizzas. Soon we got him caught up and the night hummed along, with two coworkers in the front room making sandwiches and serving up soups and veggie-rice casseroles from steam trays behind the counter, Glen in back making pizzas, and Gretel and I keeping up with the dishes. As the work slowed, we noticed a slew of pots and pans piled high in a deep utility sink, so we started in on those.

After the restaurant closed, we sat in the dining room drinking sweet, bright carrot juice and eating heaps of their famed super rice casserole (brown rice with all kinds of vegetables, cheese, and a luscious cream sauce). Glen offered us jobs as dishwashers.

For possibly the first time in my life, I felt wildly cool.

When I arrived for my first night of work, once again full dish tubs had overtaken the dishwashing area. It was only 5:00 p.m., and it looked like Steven (a guy in his midtwenties who managed the place on weeknights) was already in over his head.

I immediately got to work.

"Wait!" said Steven. He opened the door of the walk-in cooler. "How 'bout some malted barley juice?" he called from inside.

"Sure," I said, steeling myself for a flavor I wasn't sure I'd love.

He walked out of the cooler, opened a can of beer, grabbed the last two clean glasses, and evenly split the beer between them.

"Cheers," he said, handing me a glass.

He asked me a couple of questions: If I wanted something to eat, what kind of music I wanted him to play during my shift? But soon the string of brass bells on the front door jingled and a group of customers came in. "We'll talk some more later," he said as he went out front.

The night got busier than I'd ever seen as a customer. People sat on the window ledges, reading alternative newspapers from elsewhere and waiting for tables while Steven took orders, prepared them, and served them. Rick, an amazingly cute student at Drake, came in at 6:00 to make pizzas, manning the phone orders and to-go pickups from out the back door. They both got so busy that they put me in charge of the music, and I got so busy that I simply kept flipping the cassette of Bob Dylan's *Desire* from one side to another.

At one point, I was all caught up on dishes, but Steven still had a few order chits lined up. I saw that the metal pans of raw ingredients he needed to make the sandwiches were getting low. Rick set up a little station for me to chop and slice and grate some ingredients, catch-as-catch-can.

"Where's the fire?" Rick said at one point. "Really—just mellow out."

I couldn't help having a sense of urgency. I'd worked in enough restaurants to know that we were, in restaurant-speak, "in the weeds," which meant you were hopelessly behind in ways you'd have night-mares about for the rest of your life.

But each time I brought the prepped ingredients out to Steven's sandwich station, I'd take a glance at the dining room. At first, I'd inwardly wince that some of the customers I'd seen a long while before still didn't have their food. Then I realized that, as they sat there talking in low murmurs and sipping pineapple-coconut juice and listening to *Desire* amid this microcosm of everything that was good about the world in those days, everyone seemed just fine.

And the food? Okay, so never mind that carob tasted like wax, and bean spread/bean sprout sandwiches on heavy whole-wheat bread sometimes had me craving a hot dog. The menu might seem a bit earnest and basic when today, there's gochujang and coconut milk, miso paste and kimchi readily available to make meatless dining truly sing. But back then, it all tasted fresh and novel and wholesome. I still crave the Soup Kitchen's broccoli soup, the super rice, and gorgeous sparkling salads with vegetables that truly tasted of themselves. I loved raw vegetable juice so much I bought a Champion juicer.

Not surprisingly, there was little hierarchy in place at the Soup Kitchen. I might have officially been the dishwasher, but soon I became the front counter order taker and started making everything from sandwiches and salads to the sought-after pizzas. If something needed doing, you did it. If I had to run the front while Steven buzzed out to replenish some cheese, the cute pizza maker would wash dishes. Everyone bussed tables; everyone scrubbed counters.

And if you didn't get that, you didn't last long. A piece of paper taped by the phone had the names and phone numbers of kids my age who had come in asking for jobs. Some who actually got the call might be disappointed that even a cool job with cool people at the coolest place in Des Moines might entail scrubbing away some gunk here and there.

Having worked in restaurants since I was thirteen and three-quarters, the fact that the work was real and sometimes even messy did not surprise me in the least. It was a restaurant, after all.

Instead of the ugly brown-and-white checkered uniform and corny bandana I had worn at Country Kitchen, I could wear blue jeans and T-shirts to work, and during slow times, we could sip half a can of cheap, watery beer and talk about *Zen and the Art of Motorcycle Maintenance* or the virtues of vegetarianism and whether we should be eating chocolate or carob. Or sometimes we'd just tell jokes or make fun of each other's tastes in music—each of us taking turns making the others listen to bands we loved to prove our own good taste. (I liked Queen. My coworkers did not. They remained unconvinced. I didn't care, because I was already in their inner circle.)

I felt worlds away from the other restaurants I had worked in, restaurants sometimes run by old-school boss ladies and imperious almost-middle-aged men and occasioned by people my parents' age who treated me like the hopelessly green youth that I was. When I was within the walls of that old storefront building, I could actually convince myself that the Soup Kitchen was a kind of utopia, or at least its own wonderful little self-contained world.

And then one day, those two worlds collided.

On a late Saturday afternoon in spring, a middle-aged woman dressed in, of all things, a smart houndstooth suit, walked in and stared at the menu overhead. Likely seeing nothing that struck her fancy, she asked if we served tuna salad sandwiches.

A little too high, I think, on the righteousness of vegetarianism and the hipness of this world that lay so far out of the realm of smart houndstooth suits, I told her we did not serve tuna fish.

"We are a *vegetarian* restaurant," I stated, emphatically.

"I am aware of that," she said politely. "But, some vegetarians do eat fish." Her kind smile faded along with, I imagine, her hope that she'd chosen the right place to eat.

"Sorry. No fish here," I said, likely with a shrug.

While I felt a pang of guilt as she turned and walked away, the memory saddens me even more with each year that passes. I often think how easy it would have been for me to make her feel welcome. All it would have taken was to suggest a sandwich she might like, grilled cheese or avocado-veggie or egg salad.

I knew that any of the real adults who worked at the Soup Kitchen would have done just about anything to make the lady in the checkered suit feel at home. Good heavens—they probably would have walked across the street and bought her a steak if she wanted one. For if there was any thread that linked the Soup Kitchen to the other, more square restaurants of its time, it was that nobody ever mistreated customers. They didn't even *complain* about customers, even when well out of earshot.

Looking back, I think there was an overall understanding among those of us who worked at the Soup Kitchen that there would be plenty of people who would walk in the door and feel out of place in our small slice of infinitely cool but (in truth) waning counterculture. The ethos was firm: everyone was welcome in this club.

No one had to explain this to me; it was as organic as the carrots I peeled and juiced day after day—which was why the tuna-fish lady's disappointment pained me so much: *I knew better*.

I soon left the Soup Kitchen; I was headed off to college and needed to make some real money. I went back to waitressing for tips, making two to three times more than the Soup Kitchen could pay me. Yet my time there made me a better server. Tuna-fish lady's look of defeat as she turned and walked out of the restaurant was something I never wanted to see again.

Many years later, when I had the great luck to report on the ever-evolving restaurant scene, I watched food get more worldly, energetic, and ambitious than anything we had in the late 1970s. But what always, *always*, moved me most was when I encountered that food along with the Glens and Graces and Stevens of today's restaurant world: those who wanted, above all, to give everyone who walked through their doors a sense of well-being, of being included, and of being cared for and in good hands during their stretch of time at the table, that all-too-brief reprieve from an indifferent world.

REFLECTIONS ON SERVICE IN
AN IMPERFECT WORLD

I wish I could say that service in the restaurants I reviewed always offered the great combination of graciousness and expertise I found at Bistro 43 and the inclusivity I had witnessed years earlier at the Soup Kitchen, as well as the everlasting friendliness and cheer we brought to our days at Baker's. Alas, that was not always the case. Service was all over the map—from inexpert to exceedingly expert, from indifferent to wholly gracious.

While finding careless or inexperienced service at a fine-dining venue could be mildly annoying, it mostly made me sad. In the handsome dining room of a lavishly renovated rural Iowa hotel, a server once told our table that the special appetizer that night was "frah gwah." She read this from a list of items she had tucked in her order pad.

She meant to say "foie gras" (pronounced "fwah grah"), and while I know sophisticates who might have snickered at her mispronunciation, I felt for her. Who had put this server in the unfair and demeaning position of serving dishes so foreign to her that she didn't have any idea how to pronounce them? Had she ever known the joy of even trying this and other dishes on the lavish menu? I also thought it unfortunate that the restaurant—smack dab in the center of rural Iowa, and designed to celebrate its history and setting—was, at that time, serving foie gras and other overwrought dishes inspired by faraway places. Fortunately, they would later move to regionally inspired food.

But she was congenial enough, and efficient (if inexpert) at her job. That was surprisingly common with servers I encountered, especially in the earliest days of reviewing: the chefs were continually raising the standards, but service lagged a few steps behind. Sometimes it was downright cringeworthy. At one otherwise ambitious restaurant, when a server came to clear our plates, rather than asking if we'd finished, she looked down at whatever was left on our plates, wrinkled her nose, and said, "Is it dead yet?"

Sometimes, an easygoing vibe I generally loved could lead to an overfamiliarity that I didn't. Once, a server in a restaurant pointed to a brand-new top I was wearing and said, "Nice top! Did you get that at Banana Republic? I work there!" When I told her I did, she said, "Well, I hope you didn't pay full price, because it's on sale now."

During the meal, I thought more often than I should have about the fact that I had overpaid for my pretty new garment.

Servers rarely knew how to keep track of silverware; when it came to desserts, some places that should have been further evolved nevertheless remained "save your fork" kind of spots. If the server happened to have taken your fork, and you happened to ask for another for your dessert, she'd often bring you an entire roll of silverware, complete with an extra knife and spoon and cloth napkin—detritus that clogged up the table.

Too often, the check was plopped down in the middle of a table filled with uncleared plates and empty cocktail glasses. Or, the server would ask us if we wanted dessert while we were still eating our entrées, or checks were brought before dessert was finished.

I tried to be forgiving of such missteps because I knew the issue lay not with the server but with management. In these cases, no one had taken the time and care to properly show waitstaff the ins and outs of table service. Or maybe someone had, but no one was there, night after night, to maintain a sense of decorum. Over the fifteen years I reviewed restaurants, I saw fewer and fewer of those old-school keen-eyed maître d's or managers circling the dining rooms; it became more common for servers to run their own sections, with no one to keep standards high or step in when things got hairy.

I once asked my friend Stephen Volkmer-Jones, a long-time restaurant industry professional, about the prime rib cart at Guido's. Located in the Savery Hotel, with plush half-moon booths, white tablecloths, and the tuxedoed proprietor running the place, this was the finest downtown restaurant in the 1980s and early 1990s. Stephen had worked there as a maître d' for many years, and his recollections spoke to how much things had changed by the late 1990s and early 2000s:

The stainless-steel and rosewood prime rib cart was a big feature at Guido's. The cart was wheeled as near to the table as possible. At first only Guido carved. Then he taught me how he wanted it done. He watched over my shoulder for two years until he felt I knew all I needed to know about it. The night he let me carve on my own was a milestone of trust.

Where did that level of front-of-the-house exactitude go? For the most part, by the mid-2000s, it had vanished, along with the maître d', whose role was replaced by the door hostess. She (and it usually *was* a she) was a beautiful young woman welcoming people from the hostess stand, then seating them and returning to the hostess stand to simply stand there and look lovely until the next party arrived. Although exceedingly pleasant and welcoming, she was not the person who would keep an eye on the entire scene, noticing when plates needed clearing here or another round of drinks needed to be ordered there.

I once made the mistake of thinking that the host of a restaurant might be able to help our table with an issue. When the wine in our glasses reeked of dishwashing detergent, and our waiter was nowhere to be found, I flagged down a host (this time, it was a young man) as he passed by and I told him of the issue. He sniffed the glass and said, "Oh! That's horrible! I wouldn't drink out of that glass!" He put the glass back down on the table and walked away. I don't think it even occurred to him that he could or should do something to help us.

I began to notice over the years that sometimes restaurant service had become likewise compartmentalized, everyone doing a job separate from everyone else, with servers almost seeming like sole-proprietor subcontractors working their sections, often with no one in charge keeping it all together. One reason for this, I've learned, is that restaurant managers are increasingly hard to find and retain. More than one-third of managers quit after a year, often due to work-life balance issues. Restaurateurs have also told me they often do have managers working the floor, but they get pulled in so many directions (even, if necessary, into the kitchen when other team members don't show up) that diners sometimes simply don't see them.

While I do miss seeing someone in charge, I don't miss the kind of formality that a reserved and decorous tuxedoed maître d' signals. I appreciate the more approachable style of today's more professional servers. Fortunately, that sniffy waiter of the 1980s and early 1990s is, for the most part, long gone.

In the very best places—the cream-of-the-crop spots where the staff were well versed in the ins and outs of table service—a new kind of top-notch server had arrived. Confident but never condescending, they effected that glad-to-be-here, glad-you're-here vibe that I so loved at Bistro 43. As food became a national obsession, the best servers began to be much more than order takers and plate deliverers: they were deft, reassuring, and highly knowledgeable about the food and wines they served. The best were also your collaborators. When they'd listen to you and you'd listen to them, together you could coax the best meal possible out of the kitchen. It didn't happen all the time, but it was sheer delight when it did—when service finally caught up with the kitchen's ambitions.

Once in a while I'd encounter the new-millennium descendent of those '80s style of waiters, but by then haughtiness had been replaced with a kind of know-it-all-ness. I remember once while looking over a menu at a restaurant, I turned to a tablemate and said, "Oh! They have bucatini all'Amatriciana!" In my excitement over spotting one of my favorite dishes on the menu, I might have forgotten that a "c" in Italian is never sibilant; that is, a "c" is never pronounced as an "s."

A waiter, filling up the water glasses at the other side of the table, butted in. "Excuse me?" he said. He then stood there, quite dramatically, waiting for us to halt our conversation and give him our full attention. "It's pronounced 'all'ah-mah-tree-CHA-nuh.'"

I really wanted to say, "Pardon me? I wasn't talking to you." But answering rudeness with more rudeness has always made me feel worse than better. I let it go, but like the little boy at Country Kitchen whose family made fun of him for the "peek-in pie," I was a bit crestfallen, more than I should have been as an adult—at least until a stiff drink and great conversation got the evening back on track.

I later thought of the lady in the houndstooth suit I had been so rude to at the Soup Kitchen all those years before. Suddenly, I had become that uncool middle-aged customer, with a young waiter quick to point out just how uncool I was. It's true: what goes around comes around, especially in the world of cool.

When reviewing restaurants, I often wondered how much I should let a rude waiter affect my review. Shouldn't I just put my ego in a suitcase and focus on the food? After all, most diners can shrug off rudeness.

But they shouldn't have to.

Again, my loyalty was to my reader. Sometimes I would even envision how regular (non-expense-account-abetted) customers might feel in a given situation. When it came to service, I often thought of my friends Bruce and Marcia. Both worked in nonprofits and loved great food but didn't have a lot of money to splash around on dining out. One year on their anniversary, they went to one of the splurgiest restaurants in town—a venue that I had, in fact, praised in an earlier review. The food was good, they told me. Really good. "But our waiter—he was so condescending. He made us feel like we didn't belong," said Marcia.

Imagine the glum feeling of coming home after an overpriced evening where you were made to feel "less than" rather than like a valued guest. Imagine this on a night you had saved up for and set aside for the sole purpose of celebrating your shared happiness. Imagine wondering over the years if you should even dare to go out to dinner again and risk the possibility of another lousy experience, another lousy memory, on your anniversary.

The greatest insults are easy to report and long remembered. Once, as a student, I went into a bar-grill in Iowa City for an early lunch. It was a seat-yourself venue, so I sat down at the smallest table I could find (a two-top) in the casual, near-empty restaurant. Soon after the server took my order, the owner came up and asked me if I was dining alone. I told him yes, I was. He then requested that I move to a stool at the bar (alongside a bunch of day-drinkers) so that the table would be available for two diners when the restaurant filled up during the lunch rush. I got up and left the restaurant, in a houndstooth-suit-lady kind of way.

A couple years later, a few months after I had moved to New York, my father and mother came to visit. More than anything, Dad wanted to have dinner at the Rainbow Room. We met Dave (then boyfriend, now husband) for dinner on the sixty-fifth floor of 30 Rockefeller Plaza, where we were seated at white-clothed tables, surrounded by views of the glittering city amid an aged crowd of mostly (I imagine) out-of-towners.

Mom and Dad were wonderful dancers and spent as much of the evening as they could gliding across the dance floor to Sy Oliver's band. They'd come back to the table, flushed and giddy at their good fortune of dining and dancing on top of the world.

"Who wouldn't want to be us?" my mother said at one point. It was a phrase she often used whenever we were lucky enough to be doing something marvelous in a marvelous place.

The food was fine enough, but the service was cool and haughty in the way fine-dining service often was in the 1980s. My father hadn't had a drink since the early 1950s, and our imposing late-middle-aged server likely rolled his eyes when Dad ordered coffee with his meal and then kept requesting that his cup be refilled throughout the evening.

After dessert, the server asked us if we'd like some after-dinner drinks. A Cognac perhaps? Getting up to take another spin on the dance floor with Mom, Dad encouraged Dave and me to order whatever we wished. Cognac sounded nice.

When the bill came, I happened to glance at it. The two Cognacs cost something like twenty dollars, the equivalent of nearly sixty dollars in today's money. I apologized to my father; I knew it would have been more prudent to ask for a drinks menu instead of letting a waiter cajole me into such an expensive option.

My father shook his head, shrugging off my apology, and playfully tossed his credit card on the little silver tray with a huge grin. Absolutely nothing was going to ruin his night. Until he died, he would often talk about the fun we all had at the Rainbow Room, never once mentioning the expense of it or the waiter's blatant upsell. But I never forgot. If he wasn't a bit disappointed, I was disappointed for him.

Like my father, most of the midwestern diners I wrote for could shrug such things off. They shouldn't have to.

Reporting on bad service was one of the hardest things to get down on paper. There's a certain "Iowa nice" ethos out there that makes you feel kind of ridiculous grousing about uncleared plates. A typical midwestern comment I occasionally received when I mentioned subpar service was, "First world problems!" Even now, as I write this, I imagine some readers thinking, *Oh, boo-hoo. With all the troubles in the world, you're concerned about Bruce and Marcia having a snooty waiter, about your dad getting snookered by a server forty years ago?*

Yes, I am. All the problems in a messed-up world do not excuse restaurants from doing right by the diners who have trusted them with their hard-earned money, hard-won leisure time, and memories of a night they will either think back on with a smile or a wince.

And then there's this: with all the troubles in the world, maybe the table is a place where for just a little while, you can feel that all *is* right in the world, at least in your world. Yes, it's a lot to ask, but those in the restaurant industry have more power than they may realize to make such a thing happen. This is just one of the many lessons I learned about doing right by our guests—and each other—when I worked among the dedicated pros at the Younkers department-store restaurants.

RAREBIT BURGERS AND STICKY BUNS

"Hash-slinging" was my father's disparaging term for restaurant work. He himself had owned a small-town café—Shoppe's Café in Jefferson, Iowa—after finishing two tours of duty in the European Theatre of World War II. He left the restaurant business to become a salesman long before I was born and had no enduring love for restaurant work whatsoever. I'm not even sure he liked to go out to eat that much.

After my stint at Country Kitchen, I thought maybe Dad was right: hash-slinging was no business to be in. I applied for a seasonal job wrapping Christmas gifts at a Younkers department store in the Merle Hay Mall, a gleaming, ever-growing sprawl that began as an outdoor shopping plaza in 1959. By the 1970s, it had become a flourishing, fully covered mall, complete with smoke-tinted skylights and tropical plants towering over white plastic flat-dish fountains, on the suburban edges of the north side of Des Moines.

My timing was sheer luck. The old personnel department manager who took my application hired me on the spot, with barely a few words by way of an interview, and told me to start work in two weeks. I have no idea why she hired me so spontaneously, but her doing so changed my life, eventually leading me to a job I would hold pretty much throughout high school and college, and the memory of which I will cherish as long as I live.

When I showed up to report to work on my first day, the old manager was no longer there. The clerk in the personnel office told me that the woman had retired the week before. Furthermore, no one could find any record of my being hired at all—there had been a hiring freeze that, in fact, the woman disregarded. As I sat in the waiting room while they wondered what to do with me, someone must have taken pity on my crestfallenness. They told me that, for the moment, the store had all the gift-wrappers they needed, but they would assign me to Men's Furnishings. I had no idea what "Men's Furnishings" was, but I was soon selling shirts, ties, gloves, pajamas, robes, and colognes four nights a week from 5 to 9 p.m.

It was nice to wear real clothes instead of a uniform, and style my hair rather than flattening it underneath a bandana. It was even better to smell like men's cologne rather than prep oil when I left work. Trouble was, after the constant hustle of restaurant work, standing behind a counter selling colognes and ties was *boring*. While the early evening was busy enough, during that interminably slow stretch between 7 p.m. and when I clocked out at 9, the hours dragged. There were only so many times you could dust the counters, refold shirts, and straighten the tie case. I would entertain myself by playing with a calculator, trying to see how close I could come to guessing what, say, 143 times 275 would equal.

I also really missed the tips. At Younkers I made more per hour than I had waiting tables. But with no tips, the pay ended up being a good 50 percent less than what I had made with tips at Country Kitchen. Meanwhile, a high school chum named Deb, who worked upstairs at the Younkers Meadowlark Room (the department store's highly popular restaurant), would stop by my men's cologne counter after the restaurant closed at 8:00 p.m. and complain how her purse was *so* heavy because of *all her tips*.

Like a novice vegetarian who still salivates after a juicy hamburger, I couldn't shake my yearning for hash-slinging in general and working for tips in particular. After a scant few months working in Men's Furnishings, I rode the escalator up to the second floor, past the desks of the knife- and scissor-sharpener and the sewing-machine repairmen, and applied for a job at the Meadowlark Room. My five-second interview was with managers Wilma and Gladys, two chain-smoking women in their fifties. They were the type of commanding, nononsense women who my father would sometimes refer to—quite respectfully—as battle-axes. After learning that I'd done this all before and was actually willing to sign up to do it again, their only question was, "When can you start?"

When I told my father about the new job, he shook his head and warned, "Once a hash-slinger, always a hash-slinger." He knew how hard the habit was to break, and I think he was a little worried that I'd become a lifer. Yet my parents approved of the shorter hours—4:30 to 8:00 p.m.—and we all intuited correctly that working for the tough-but-fair lady bosses at the Meadowlark would have little in common with working for the almost-middle-aged men at Country Kitchen.

And so I went to work, slinging the famed Younkers rarebit burgers (hamburgers draped in cheese sauce), sticky buns (small cinnamon rolls topped with a generous pat of butter served with every non-sandwich meal), signature chicken salads, frosty malts, butterscotch-meringue ice cream balls, the popular potato salad with its pink-hued dressing, and other yearned-for Younkers specialties.

Most everything was made in-house from scratch, or if not, a daily delivery of homemade soups, salads, casseroles, roasts, and baked goods arrived from the vast kitchens of the Younkers Tea Room on the top floor of the flagship store downtown. While Country Kitchen was a place where (aside from burgers and breakfasts) many things were assembled, not really cooked and probably not baked, at Younkers even things that other restaurants sourced from large food-service companies were instead made in-house, right down to the biscuits for our chicken à la king and the mayonnaise for the chicken salad.

Our soups were legendary and usually followed a weekly schedule—a thick Yankee bean soup with chunks of meaty ham hock on Tuesdays; a fresh and sprightly tomato-based vegetable soup on Saturdays; clam chowder on Fridays—with "white" and "red" (New England and Manhattan, respectively) alternating weekly.

These were the salad bar years, when nearly every respectable restaurant had one. Yet few rivaled ours. It was loaded with our homemade salads, like pea, three-bean, and kidney bean; the famous five-cup salad with pineapples, mandarin oranges, and coconut; and tossed salads and trimmings, including our famous Teton dressing (their own brand of creamy garlic dressing). The first time I ever saw a garbanzo bean was on that salad bar.

The Meadowlark's specialty, however, was the prime rib dinner, served nightly after 4:30 p.m. For $2.90, you got a trip through the salad bar, a choice of vegetable and potato (baked, mashed, or au gratin), Younkers sticky buns, and a formidable slab of prime rib that had been slow-roasted in-house.

Even in the late 1970s, $2.90 was shockingly cheap for a prime rib dinner. I was told that it was priced as a loss leader to get foot traffic into the store, and it worked. Night after night, people would line up and happily wait—sometimes even thirty minutes or so—to get seated. It was a brilliant ploy, as usually one person in the party would hold a place in line while the others wandered the store, often coming back with a purchase or two.

The dining room itself was the nicest I'd worked in yet. It was a few leaps above a cafeteria or coffee shop, a few smaller steps down from fine dining. Though the handsome wood tables were topped with paper placemats rather than tablecloths, the room was carpeted in a luminous gold-and-brown design, and the décor included charming Audubon-esque illustrations of grassland birds, like the meadowlark for whom the restaurant was named.

The room might have been refined, but some of the kids I worked with were a little rough around the edges. Some of the busboys, dishwashers, and line cooks would occasionally get high in the men's dressing room. Now and then a young waitress or two hid a pint of booze in the women's dressing room and popped in for nip during a slow stretch. And everyone—I mean everyone—smoked cigarettes.

Me? I did not drink at work—not out of any kind of morality, but because I wanted to be on my game to make the most in tips I could. Outside of work, however, I did all the things that most seventeen-year-olds I knew did at the time: smoked a few cigarettes, puffed on a joint if one happened to come my way at a party, and put a half-pint of amber Bacardi in my purse to share with friends, adding the booze to cups of soft drinks with crushed ice when we played in the pep band at high school games. Until mid-1978, our state's drinking age was eighteen, and anyone who looked about sixteen and a half could buy alcohol from the state-run liquor stores, staffed—I now surmise—by aging men, many of them World War II and Korean vets who likely knew damned well how old we were, but who had probably seen much worse things in their lives than an underage kid buying a half-pint of booze for kicks.

I suspect that Wilma and Gladys had seen worse, too. Wilma once said, as she waved an empty pint bottle of Ten High she had found in the women's dressing room, "Between the boys and their dope and the girls and their hooch, I suppose one of these days I'll have to call security to help me clean house."

But as long as the cooks kept good food coming out of the kitchen, the dishwashers kept plenty of clean dishes and silverware stocked, and the front of the house kept the customers happy, Wilma forgave a lot. In fact, she once told us that there were many things she would overlook; she understood that orders got mixed up, glasses got shattered, soft drinks got spilled. But she would never, ever forgive us for being rude to anyone who sat at our tables or rude to each other. And she forbade us to give anyone the stink eye for coming in to be seated at the stroke of closing time—or even a few minutes afterward.

Wilma often said reliable help was hard to find. If you showed up to work on time and you were willing to work hard when you got there, she treated you well. And she worked every bit as hard as she expected you to. She'd be on the floor or in the kitchen every minute of the mealtime rushes. I can still see her on those nights when the cooks fell behind. She'd don a spattered cook's apron over her well-tailored dress and work right alongside them, flipping burgers, plating prime rib, dishing up chicken à la king, with her cigarette dangling from her lips, her steel-gray hair perfectly coiffed in one of those ratted-and-teased styles of the time, her battle-axe-itude coming out in full force as she hustled the kitchen back into shape.

Out on the floor (sans cigarette and apron), she oversaw the dining room with a keen eye, not only touching tables and glad-handing but also stepping in when a plate needed clearing, a coffee cup needed filling, a customer needed placating, or an errant waitress needed rounding up from dillydallying too long, flirting with the line cooks in the kitchen.

One day, in the middle of a lunch shift, she found me standing in the back of the dish room, holding a plate up to my face, shoving massive bites of one of those famous rarebit burgers into my mouth.

"For heaven's sake—sit down and eat that thing or you'll choke on it," she said, agreeing to watch my tables for a few minutes while I sat in a back room. When I got back on the floor and thanked her, she said to me, "Well, you can't wait tables very well on an empty stomach, now can you? And next time, for God's sake, sit down and eat something like the rest of us before you get on the floor."

Before that, I had sometimes neglected to get to work in time for our optional preshift meal, but Wilma convinced me to start being part of the ritual. She knew I'd appreciate serving good food to our customers if I myself had been likewise nourished. But even more important, it seemed she really wanted me to be part of this employee meal.

Even before the pandemic, the turnover rates in the hospitality industry were astronomical (according to the National Restaurant Association, the turnover rate in the restaurants and accommodations sector was nearly 75 percent in 2018). During the years I worked at the Younkers Meadowlark, while the teens would come and go, many adults working in both the kitchen and dining rooms remained steady. It was a different time in so many ways: Younkers offered benefits to full-time employees, and the managers treated the staff with respect. In return, most everyone did their jobs not with resentment or resignation (as I had first seen at Country Kitchen), but with old-school pride and expertise day after day, year after year.

Fifty-somethings Anna and Irene were servers of an ilk we'll likely never see again. What always struck me most, even back in those days when anyone over twenty was practically invisible to me, was their professionalism. Some days I'd barely comb my hair before throwing on the stupid hairnet I had to wear, but Anna and Irene were always flawlessly groomed, with washed-and-set hair; neat manicures; impeccably applied rouge, face powder, and lipstick; and perfect bows on the backs of their aprons. Even though all uniforms were professionally washed and ironed at the end of every day, I would sometimes spot Irene re-pressing her uniform in the dressing room before her shift because it just wasn't crisp enough. My white waitress shoes would often be so crusted over with spilled food that Wilma would have to remind me to wipe them off and blot them with the shoe whitener she kept in her office, but Anna's and Irene's shoes were always spotless.

Both had worked at the Meadowlark for so long and were so well respected that regular customers would request their tables. They took especially good care of regular customers who were store clerks working in other departments of Younkers or other stores at the mall. Knowing that clerks' breaks were limited, Irene and Anna would take their orders the minute they sat down, then try to hustle the food from the kitchen as quickly as possible.

A former Younkers manager recently gifted me a little booklet, the *Younkers Tea Room Waitress Manual*. It was written and used long before either of us ever worked for Younkers restaurants, but its overall ethos endured well into our time there. On the first page is written:

> *Art is the doing of anything well. It's not the thing itself, but how it is done that counts. All customers are our guests and our entire attention should be given to their comfort and convenience. We want the atmosphere of our tea room to be restful and full of cheer so that our guests may go away happier for having dined with us.*

I don't know if Anna or Irene ever read this manual from the Meadowlark's sister restaurant, but it seems to me they took these words to heart. I am sure most everyone they served went away happier for having dined at their tables.

The two had even earned their own sections; that is, they never rotated through the Back One, Back Two, or Back Three clusters of tables assigned to the rest of us. They had eponymous territories, named "Anna's" and "Irene's"—premium sections with the best tables in the restaurant. You knew you had risen up the ranks when you were assigned to work either Anna's or Irene's on one of their nights off or on Sunday (which neither ever worked).

While most tips those days were in loose change—fifty cents for a table of two was considered good—I'd often spot dollar bills left on Anna's and Irene's tables. It was then that I realized there was a knack to this job. I started watching what they did and picking up a few hints that now seem obvious, like clearing plates in a timely manner or waiting to bring the check to the table until the customer was done eating rather than slapping it down the minute I delivered dessert. Cooks knew not to be sloppy with any of Anna's or Irene's orders—they wouldn't stand for skimpy portions or spattered plates.

I noticed that Anna and Irene would do things that their customers would not even realize had been done for them. They would preheat the individual coffee or teapots by pouring hot water into them, letting them sit for a moment, then emptying and refilling them with hot water or coffee. Both would inspect glasses for the soft drinks before filling them—if they were cloudy or spotted from the dishwasher, they'd keep poking around for one that sparkled.

I don't know what happened to Anna, but Irene passed away some time ago. I learned this when, after I had mentioned in a story I wrote for the *Des Moines Register* that I had worked at the Meadowlark, a man wrote to me to tell me that his mother, who had passed away, had spent many years working at the Meadowlark. Her name was Irene. He told me he had fond memories of being taken by his father to the restaurant for a meal once or twice when he was a youngster.

I remember thinking, *How sad—your mother worked there all those years and you only ate there once or twice?* But then it hit me: Anna and Irene worked their jobs with the kind of rigor and dignity that left no room for their kids coming in to disrupt the seamless functioning of their sections. They were not just old school, they were ancient school—relics of a past that even their own childhoods may have only skirted. They would have been well suited to roles on the staffs of the grand European estates of another era.

I'm glad servers today need not be so servant-like. Still, looking back, I admire their spirit and dedication. Never mind that Anna and Irene were not waiting on earls and countesses but rather on middle-class shoppers piling in for the $2.90 prime rib special. It didn't matter, because as a customer, your contract with them was this: when you sat at their tables, you were always treated like you deserved the best. You were always in good hands.

Unfortunately, not everyone was as professional as Irene and Anna. Every place has its bully, and over the years I worked at the Meadowlark, a few rotated in and out, generally among the kitchen staff. One was a nineteen-year-old cook who had worked at the Meadowlark throughout high school; he had now graduated and was trying to decide what to do with his life while making ends meet with evening shifts on the line.

Bill often had some sort of dirty joke to play on you or something filthy to say. He'd tell a waitress, "Gee, you have the whitest teeth I've ever come across," and wait for you to smile. Hardy-har-har. And if you were too smart to fall for the venereal joke, if you said something like, "In your dreams," you'd fear he'd be resentful, holding back your orders behind others that came later when Wilma wasn't looking.

When a young waitress was gone for a couple weeks, recovering, we were told, from appendicitis, Bill said, as he coolly chewed on a toothpick, "Bullshit. She's had an abortion." Never mind that he was both cruel and most likely wrong.

Happily, the adults in the front and back of the house kept Bill and a few others like him in line. And for the most part, Bill and his buddies were the exceptions among the younger staff, who, while certainly not by any means innocent and clean-cut, were mostly good-natured kids, in spite of a little weed in the dressing rooms now and then.

While I enjoyed working for the fair-minded battle-axes at the Meadowlark Room and truly loved making tips, about a year and a half into my first stint, I gave notice. It was my fourth Saturday in a row working the counter, and I hit a wall.

For those who were dining alone or others who simply didn't want to wait in line for a table, the rectangular-shaped, sixteen-stool counter was a great option. Kids also preferred the counter. Kids also never tipped.

Customers in a hurry always chose the counter. Trouble was, time-pressed customers never quite understood that just because you were seated more quickly at the counter didn't mean your food would come up any faster. Not only would my tips suffer (this was way before the days of no-fault tipping), but I'd sometimes get crabbed at, too. In front of fifteen other people.

Anyone who has ever waited tables knows that it's easier to wait on four tables of four than sixteen individual diners, all in various stages of their dining experience. This guy needs a check, those two kids still want their frosty malt and plate of fries. And yikes, this lady hasn't gotten her iced tea yet and her entrée is up and waiting in the window. Plus twelve more people need something or will at any minute. And look at all those half-empty coffee cups waiting for refills.

I now suspect that on Saturdays, the counter was the busiest and hardest place to work—which was why Gladys and Wilma would assign one of their quickest and most nimble servers who was also low enough in the hierarchy not to complain. Which would have been me.

Generally, I could handle it. But that Saturday lunch, I was in the weeds. Sixteen people, including quite a few crabby old bats, were staring at me, all looking for something. Walking from the kitchen to the counter with a bowl of soup on a tray, I paused for a half second, trying to remember which crabby old bat was supposed to get the soup.

"Bring me that soup, *right now*," the bat in question yelled. I must have shaken a moment, because just then, some drops of her soup sloshed a bit onto the rim of the bowl.

"What a mess!" she said as I set it down in front of her.

And of course, as I reached down into the silverware racks below the counter for a spoon for her soup, I was, at that very moment, out of soup spoons.

Before I could say anything, she said, "Am I supposed to eat this with my hands?"

It went on from there. Working a counter is a bit like today's social media; when the outrage starts, it can gain momentum, turning quickly into a pile-on. That day, my counter became a rage machine, and I was the target. At least it felt that way to seventeen-year-old me.

At the end of the day, as we were sitting around smoking cigarettes and drinking coffee (the cool kids didn't drink soda anymore), some of the other teenage waitresses were comparing tips (mature waitresses, like Anna and Irene, would never do such a thing). Most of the girls had made between $7 and $10. I had made $3.60.

After we finished our coffee and cigarettes, I wrote up my two-weeks' notice on a little scrap of ordering paper and speared it on the paper spindle in Wilma's windowless office.

The sad thing is, I'm sure that if I had talked to Gladys and Wilma about the difficulties I was having working the counter on Saturdays, they would have been very fair to me. But I figured if I couldn't hack the job, it was my problem (my mother's work-ethic lessons did have their downside, I suppose). I also did not yet know my value; I had no idea that the old cliché "good help is hard to find" was especially true in the restaurant business.

Besides, across town in a funky old part of the city that felt worlds away from the mall, that magical train, the Soup Kitchen—and all that was great about the 1970s—was just then leaving the station. I decided to climb aboard, if only for a while.

While I worked at the Soup Kitchen for a happy six-month stretch, I left, as I've mentioned, because I was off to college the following year and needed to make some fast money. Tips were the ticket, and Gladys and Wilma were glad to have me back.

WHEN YOU COULD ALWAYS
GO . . . DOWNTOWN

Most servers I encountered in restaurants during my years of reviewing were quite young and probably not bound to stay in the biz for too long. I get it—while in the very best cases, serving tables can be a viable way to help with skyrocketing college expenses or segue from one career to another. But it's hard work and can be a thankless job. I rarely saw anyone over thirty-five waiting tables in the restaurants I reviewed. But at the Younkers restaurants, I worked alongside people who were *not* just passing through the business—and there was something remarkable in that.

After leaving the Soup Kitchen, I continued to wait tables back at Younkers Meadowlark in the late spring and summer before I headed off to college at the University of Iowa. Wilma then promised I was welcome to work there during any and all school breaks, and even on random weekends when I'd be back in Des Moines.

On Sunday, November 5, 1978, a shattering, unbearably tragic twist of fate occurred. I was home from college that weekend to go to the Moody Blues concert in Ames on Saturday night. The next morning, I remember walking outside my parents' house and looking northward. The sky was filled with billowing black clouds of smoke.

Younkers at the Merle Hay Mall was on fire, and you could see the smoke from most anywhere in the city. Ten employees, mostly office and maintenance workers who had come to work long before the store was to open at noon, perished. Fortunately, the crew who were prepping in the Meadowlark kitchen that morning managed to escape by breaking a thick glass window in the women's dressing room. Though the restaurant was on the second floor, there was another one-story building just beneath it, and the five workers were able to jump to safety without major injuries.

The store itself was a total loss, and so, I figured, was the job Wilma had promised she'd hold for me during my breaks from college. Fortunately, however, any displaced worker from the Meadowlark could get a job at the Younkers flagship store downtown. Wilma and Gladys were quickly hired on downtown, in part to help assimilate the Meadowlark staff into one of the old store's three restaurants.

In the bargain basement of the creaky old store was a casual restaurant that old-timers remembered as the Cremona Room, offering casual lunches and dinners to the sounds of a piano player tinkling out tunes near the entrance; however, in 1964, it was redesigned, sans piano player, in a midcentury orange, sage, and red color scheme and renamed simply the Coffee House. This was a casual venue—a little grubby, in fact, with seating in vinyl booths and at the Formica counter. Open for lunch and into the late afternoon, the Coffee House specialized in inexpensive short orders—burgers and sandwiches—along with soups, salads, a hot-plate special of the day, and baked goods from the Tea Room kitchen upstairs: pies, cakes, and those endearing little sticky buns.

On the street level was the Parkade Pantry. While it, too, was basically a coffee shop, it was more akin to the Meadowlark than the Coffee House. Banquette seating ran along the windows that looked out across Locust Street to the Register and Tribune Building; the rest of the room was filled with sturdy tables and dark-blonde wooden captain's chairs with canned-pea-green vinyl cushioning that matched the color of our uniforms. A small counter, complete with cake and pie cases on the wall, lined one side of the room. The Parkade Pantry opened at 7:30 in the morning, and every day it saw a breakfast rush (with eggs any way, nailed every time) and a jam-packed lunch crowd—they offered a combination of short orders and one or two more refined Tea Room specialties, such as the famed chicken salad or the fruitarian plate, with a scoop of cottage cheese surrounded by fresh fruits in a sweet and shiny poppy-seed dressing.

On the top floor was the illustrious Younkers Tea Room, the kind of venerable downtown department-store tearoom that nearly every major city had once upon a time (and profoundly misses today). The menu was pretty much the same as those of the Meadowlark and the Parkade Pantry. Customers would take the elevators, one or two of which were still operated by uniformed attendants, upstairs; they'd pile in for rarebits, chicken salads, fruitarian plates, sticky buns, and frosty malts. A few heartier specials also rotated on and off the menu, including turkey divan, chicken à la king, beef stroganoff, and other midcentury, elegant-for-the-time classics.

Even if the Tea Room's menu was similar to that of the Meadowlark Room, everything was infinitely more elegant at the Tea Room. Tables were draped with linens; round-backed chairs were plushily cushioned. Handsome square pillars soared to the high, fancifully molded ceilings from which chandeliers sparkled, while natural light streamed in from the arched French windows. Elegance was in the details, too: ketchup and mustard, for example, were always served in individual glass rame-kins placed atop paper-doily-lined plates. At the front of the room was a large stage where, in earlier decades, swing bands played at dinner dances. The stage was still used for fashion shows as well as seasonal festivities—entertainment for a Santa's brunch or a Mother's Day tea.

There existed a clear social stratification among the workers at the three downtown Younkers restaurants, and the code was easily revealed when we saw who went where. With her starched aprons and impeccable service, Irene, of course, quickly nabbed her own coveted section (by the arched French windows, naturally) at the Tea Room. Lynelle—a rough-talking twenty-something with perm-frizzled, unconvincingly dyed hair—was quickly dispatched to the Coffee House in the basement. Others were relegated along similar lines.

Me? While I was trained to work in the Tea Room and did sub there occasionally, I was permanently posted, in the summer of 1979, to the in-between realm of the Parkade Pantry.

I loved working in the ancient, timeworn store; though the old behemoth revealed a certain faded glory by the time I was working there, it had so much more character than the gleaming mall. Sometimes, when going up to the Tea Room from the ground floor, I would take a set of silent, rarely used back stairs—all terrazzo and iron and lit by the faint alley light filtered through opaque chicken-wire glass windows. Something moved me about knowing that I was part of a long line of other Younkers restaurant workers—now middle-aged, and old, and even long dead—who had been walking up and down those stairs since the 1920s.

That's probably why I always seek out the oldest restaurants in a city—institutions like Musso and Frank's in Hollywood, or the dining rooms of grand old hotels, like Parker's Restaurant in Boston's Parker House Hotel, the English Grill in Louisville's Brown Hotel, and the much-missed, now-closed Savoy Hotel and Grill in Kansas City. None of these have had the most exciting food in town, but I'm a sap for a certain gravitas, a taste of not only tradition, but of history and of the humanity and untold stories of all those who walked into the restaurant over the years, through both the front doors and back.

Though the job at the Parkade Pantry came easily, it was a world away from any place I'd worked before. Earlier restaurants I had worked in had been in mostly solid middle-class milieus on the west side or suburban north side of town. I was now working downtown, and while most of my customers were professional store clerks and office workers, occasionally unshaven down-and-out men would wander in and sit at the counter. They looked hungrier than I'd ever seen anyone in my life.

Far from being disdainful toward any of these men, servers approached them with kindness—and, I suspect, likely ensured they got a little more food on their plates than was customary. Toni, a pretty twenty-something woman with long, frosted dark-blonde hair and deep brown eyes, would approach these men with a kind of tenderness, stopping to chat when she had the time, making sure their cups were full, finding a newspaper for them to read and linger over. There was a motherly-sisterly solicitude present.

When I worked evening shifts at the Meadowlark, most workers were middle-class kids like me, saving money for college or to buy a bike or jeans and sweater sets, splurging on a big bag of cashews now and then. But working downtown meant working the day shift, and for these people the job was their livelihood. I was saving money for college expenses; their paychecks went to rent and food and diapers and car payments and inevitable car repairs. My fellow workers knew things about life I had not experienced yet.

One afternoon, a sallow-looking middle-aged man came in, wincing as he slowly and stiffly settled into a banquette by the window. When I approached to take his order, I could see sores oozing on his arm, fresh bruises blacking on his face.

"Fell off a ladder, damn the luck," the man said.

As I was putting his order in, Toni said, "That guy in your section's seen some trouble."

"Yeah," I said. "He said he fell off a ladder."

"Like hell," replied Toni. "Someone beat the crap out of him."

That she suspected such a thing, and that it hadn't even occurred to me, speaks volumes of the two different worlds we lived in.

So many of the customers I served and the people I worked with at the Parkade Pantry enlarged my view and understanding of the human condition.

Forty-something Gerald was a longtime dishwasher for Younkers. He was a quiet man with a muscular build and thinning reddish-blonde hair in Brylcreemed strands; his glasses were almost always steamed or smudged from his hot work in the dish room. He clocked in, loaded, washed, and stacked dishes for eight hours (with a half-hour meal break), then clocked out. I had never worked in a restaurant where the dishwashers were much older than teenagers, and I wondered what was keeping him in such a job. At one point, Toni, who seemed to know everything, happened to mention to me that he had a plate in his head, which I didn't quite understand.

One day, a man who resembled a dapper version of Gerald came to see him in the late afternoon. They stood by the dishwashing operation talking a while. The man stood with his arms crossed at his chest in exactly the same way I'd seen Gerald stand when things slowed down in the dish room. And then the man left.

"That was Gerald's brother," Toni whispered to me later. "He's a tax accountant."

I would work with Gerald for another three years—he moved to the suburban Meadowlark when it eventually reopened after the fire. We always exchanged cordial words—he'd ask me how school was and what I was studying; I'd ask him how he'd been doing, if anything was new at the restaurant. Over the years, I've sometimes wondered about his purported head injury. What had happened to him that made his path diverge so greatly from his brother's? It could have been something as commonplace as a childhood accident or as monumental as a war.

Then there was Ada, a hostess and a lovely young woman of about nineteen or twenty, with the blackest-black hair and a creamy complexion with rosy-pink cheeks. Honest to God, she looked more like Snow White than anyone I've ever met in my life. And she was just as sweet—one of those people who was always in a good mood. Customers could snap at her for trying to seat them at a table they didn't like, waitresses could crab at her for overloading or underloading their sections, and she'd just perk up and do whatever to help.

The only thing she wouldn't do was operate the cash register.

When Louise, the cashier—a downtown church-going lady who dressed impeccably, had her hair done weekly, and kept romance novels under the counter to read during the midafternoon lull—took her break, someone from the floor would have to run the register. Sometimes I would do it; other times another server would step in. But never Ada.

"She can't count change," Louise explained to me once. "Other than that, she can do everything else. She's a great worker."

Louise always treated Ada with the greatest kindness, encouraging her when she did well, gently correcting her when she made a mistake.

The downtown Younkers had a knack for hiring good people to work in their restaurants. Nobody blew cigarette smoke in my face; teenage cooks didn't demean waitresses with dirty innuendos. I think one thing that kept us all in line was that there was always, without fail, an eagle-eyed manager on the floor of the restaurant during the mealtime rush.

But much more than that, I had left the world of working with teenagers who needed to be reined in. Everyone employed at the downtown restaurants was an adult; there were no Ten High bottles in the women's dressing room, no smell of weed coming from the men's. And there was something real and understood in the way everyone simply wanted to do a good job and then go home.

Working the rush upstairs in the Tea Room, where I was occasionally posted if they were short-staffed, I once grabbed a plate of chicken à la king from the line before the head line cook had tucked my ticket underneath, signaling that he was thoroughly done plating it.

The plate had looked done enough to me; besides, I was in the zone, that place where servers go when we have about forty-five things in our heads to do and there's a very thin thread tying it all together, making it all work. One bad timing, one missing fork, one fruitless trip to the kitchen to check on something that was not yet there could snowball, slinging us into that nightmarish hell where nothing's going right and everyone at your table needs something *right now*.

The cook, a tall, middle-aged man dressed in his starched chef's whites came out from behind the line and took the plate from my tray, carrying it back behind the line. Jerking the plate in a circular motion with one hand, he expertly wiped the spattered rim clean with a cloth using his other hand, then grabbed a sprig of curly parsley out of the mountain of sprigs set in an ice bath, shook it off, and neatly placed it atop the dish. Only then did he tuck my order ticket underneath the plate.

While this probably took all of ten seconds, it felt like forever, a disruption to my flow; no waitress can afford to stand around for ten seconds when forty-five tasks are lining up.

For a moment, I thought he was just holding me back to toy with me a bit; I'd known cooks who did this. But then he came back out from behind the line, put a finger up between us as a preacher might gesture from a pulpit, and looked me straight in the eyes.

"There's *always* time to do things right," he said, "but *never* time to do things wrong."

Downstairs in the Parkade Pantry, the two line cooks I worked with day in and day out were equally old school. Like Anna and Irene at the Meadowlark and Louise at the Parkade Pantry cashier's stand, both women were meticulous about their appearance. Doris was a handsome, late-forty-something woman with powdered and rouged cold-cream-smooth skin, her dyed-blonde hair always professionally washed and set (employees got a nice discount at the department store's hair salon). Gloria was likely just a few years older and wore her steel-gray hair in a somewhat dated but always perfect French roll. Their white dresses were starched and pressed daily by the store's laundry service; while the waitress dresses were an utterly uncool canned-pea green (the Younkers store's official color) with a white collar and cuffs and a white apron, the cook uniforms were stiff white cotton and actually quite handsome in a nicely fitted, button-front, cuff-sleeved way.

Gloria and Doris worked seamlessly together as a pair. In the mornings, one would keep the bacon and sausage and toast going while perfectly timing each order of eggs—an intricate task when you consider that every customer wanted their eggs different (over easy; medium, hard; sunny-side up; scrambled; poached light, medium, or hard; and so on). The other would make the pancakes, grill home fries, bake waffles, and ready the sides. Lunch was similarly split, with one of them handling the burgers and hot sandwiches while the other did the salads, cold sandwiches, and blue-plate specials.

In general, the breakfast and lunch rushes went smoothly. Day in and day out, all summer, they nailed every order, every single time. I don't recall ever having to send anything back to the kitchen.

Yet every once in a while, I would notice that one of the orders I had written up for Gloria's station would strangely not appear in the window. Curiously, orders that I placed well afterward would come up, but every so often, one would invariably lag.

I would deliver the new orders out to the tables, and the customers waiting for the lagging orders—placed earlier than the ones being delivered—would follow me with their eyes every time I went back to the short-order window. I'd finally ask Gloria where the order was.

"What exactly was it for?" she'd ask.

I'd verbally tell her the order. And then she'd make it.

This didn't happen daily, but when it did, I couldn't understand it. Gloria had no reason to toy with me; we got along amicably enough. And yet every few days, I'd have this kind of trouble.

After a while, I realized that the orders that kept getting held back were ones on which I had written a special request, like the woman who wanted a rarebit burger with no top bun and with the cheese sauce on the side. Or someone who wanted a Reuben without sauerkraut (dumb request, I know). I got to thinking that Gloria simply didn't like special orders. I could understand that—when the thread of a rush is tightly wound, a special order can perilously unspool that thread. But still.

One night that summer I had the quintessential "server's dream." Anyone who's ever waited tables knows it. It's like the actor's dream, the one where you're on stage and don't know your lines. You're standing in the middle of a dining room and everything's in chaos. Countless customers all need something, but you can't seem to get your hands on the one thing someone needs most *right now*, like a fork. Someone needs a fork, and you can't find one anywhere, not in the kitchen, not in the dish room, not in the back servers' stations in the dining room. Hours are passing and you've gone on serving others; you've been able to do everything else you need to do, countless tables have turned, countless customers have come and gone, but there's still that man at a table who needs a fork, and every time you go by him, he's looking at you, waiting. You re-remember to go look for a fork. But you still can't find one. More time passes, more diners come and go, but there he is, waiting for his fork. Which you still can't find.

At one point in this dream, I'm standing at the order window and there's Gloria in the kitchen, squinting at one of my order tickets and saying, "Wini, I can't read your chicken-scratch handwriting. What's this say?"

I don't know what shuffled around in my mind, but when I woke up, a notion hit me, clear as the morning light streaming through the lacy curtains in the bedroom of my youth: *Maybe Gloria can't read?*

I thought about how Gloria would slide a batch of order tickets up off the paper spindle in the short-order window, arrange them on her counter, stare at them a moment or two, and get to work. But once in a while, she'd lean over to Doris, showing her a ticket and asking her about it. Doris would say something in return and they'd both get back to work.

When Gloria ignored one of my orders, it likely happened when Doris was away from her station. Perhaps Doris was in on the secret.

Gloria cooked smartly and efficiently, keeping on top of it all—at any given time, she could have five burgers in various states of doneness and three different kinds of sandwiches all on the griddle, keeping the French fryer going and prepping all the plates with the buns and lettuce and pickles and darting back into the walk-in to replenish the sliced onions, never missing a beat. She must have been able to make out most of the most common words in the order rotation—rarebit, fries, Reuben, eggs OM (over medium)—but perhaps not much beyond that.

Out of all the women I worked with that summer downtown, Darlene was the only one I saw outside of work. She gave me a few rides home from work, and a couple times we stopped off for a two-for-one happy hour at a nearby bar. Darlene, who had a row of freckles that ran under thick-lashed brown eyes, had worked at the Parkade Pantry long enough to have snagged her own regular section—a prime location that included many of the window tables. Unlike the newer staff, she never had to work the counter (as always, the worst section for tips and where people were always in a hurry).

In the world of waitressing, Darlene had both markets covered: like Irene in the Tea Room, she was a true professional server. I would

see her double-checking plates out of the short-order window. On
the rare occasion there was a spatter, she would ask the cook to wipe
it clean. And like Irene, Darlene was always impeccably made-up; she
wore her hair in a '70s-style close-cut Afro and she'd often steal away
to the back kitchen to freshen her lipstick.

Darlene was young and pretty. I surmised that this meant she
got tips for being professional, and that she got extra tips, especially
from men, for being easy on the eyes. Being realistic, however, I also
imagined there were some reprehensible customers who tipped her
less because of the color of her skin.

One of the marks of a truly professional server was that they never
told you how much they made in tips. While some of us would count
our change and practically sing it out loud if we reached fifteen dollars
at the end of an eight-hour shift, servers like Irene and Darlene kept
their earnings to themselves. But when circling the room, I would
sometimes see dollar bills on Darlene's table, while most of my tips
were in change.

Darlene and I had the kind of easygoing relationship that young
waitresses can effortlessly fall into. We gossiped about others we
worked with and crabbed about our manager. We spoke of boyfriend
problems; I was nursing a broken heart—I had been unspectacularly
dumped by a guy I had been crazy about at college that year.

She'd tease me about how unkempt I was when I rolled in each
morning to work. It was true: clocking in at 7:30 a.m. was tough duty
for a nineteen-year-old who'd spent the better part of the evening out
at the bars. Most mornings I'd be so perilously close to missing my
bus downtown that I'd briefly cross paths with a shower, then simply
throw on a pair of jeans and find something—anything—to wear on
top. Often it was a discarded shirt of my dad's, something unhiply
plaid or striped he'd worn many years before. Once I even showed up
wearing a flannel pajama top tucked into my jeans.

"Look at what she's wearing today!" Darlene would say as we were
getting clean uniforms out of the cupboards. Hearing Darlene laugh
was always a great way to ease into an eight-hour shift.

Later in the summer, I noticed after a few days that another server was working Darlene's prime section.

I asked Liz what happened to Darlene. She told me Darlene had resigned.

I'm not sure why I hadn't heard that Darlene was quitting; perhaps our paths hadn't crossed at opportune moments. I soon missed her, and I was sorry I wasn't able to say goodbye and wish her well. I didn't have her phone number, and I knew I couldn't just drive to her house and knock on her door—though she had given me a few rides home after work or after our two-for-one drinks, I had no idea where she lived. I had never met her other friends, nor she mine.

We had become casual friends, yet at the end of most days, aside from those drinks after work, we always went our separate ways. The random life of nineteen-year-old me just kept chugging along my path. I never saw her again.

Throughout the years I worked at Younkers restaurants, I'd sometimes encounter career waiters—men who effected the professionalism of Anna and Irene, but also brought a kind, affable, good-natured cheer to the job. I think of a guy named Cliff. When he worked the counter, he never acted like it was drudgery; rather, he *owned* that space.

"Brilliant!" I'd hear him say after taking someone's order for something as workaday as a hamburger. He'd jot down each order as if he were ending it with five exclamation points.

"Not a problem! We're easy like Sunday morning around here," he'd say when someone had a special request.

Men like Cliff were charming to everyone, but they specialized in women "of a certain age."

There was always something depressing about older women who came in and sat alone at the counter; it was as if they thought they didn't deserve to take up an entire two-top table just for themselves (businessmen and most working women, on the other hand, had no trouble doing so). Many of these women seemed like they came downtown to shop out of loneliness and little else to do. They reminded me of an older version of Audrey Hepburn's Holly Golightly wistfully window-shopping at Tiffany. Alone, the women would wander the creaky old department store's six floors—past the aging shop clerks, tape measures in their pockets waiting for the daily dribble of an equally aging clientele—before finally picking up some pantyhose or cold cream in the sundries department and having a modest lunch at the adjacent Parkade Pantry.

What a difference Cliff and waiters like him made. They never did anything stupidly condescending, like calling them "miss" instead of "ma'am." A woman would only have to order the same thing twice and they'd remember exactly how she'd liked it.

"Today, I'll have the Gizmo burger," she would say. "And I'd like it. . . ."

"Medium rare! Toasted bun! Sauce *on the side!*" the waiter would follow up in chipper staccato as if their prattle were a sweet duet in a musical.

These guys made me feel like a heel for the passive-aggressive (but harmless) stunt I'd pull now and then on a notoriously crabby customer. One young blonde woman, a buyer for the store, always came in for breakfast with a group of friends; all except Blondie would leave me at least fifteen cents or a quarter (believe it or not, standard breakfast tips at the time).

This beaky buyer—with a stringy little bowtie around her high-collared, shoulder-padded shirt and that prescient, irritatingly short, hyper-professional Leona-Hemsley-esque haircut that would take over in the '80s—would leave nothing. Not a dime. Not once. Not ever, ever, *ever*. And she was never very nice.

After a week of that (which is forever when you're nineteen), I started bringing her morning toast out with a little plastic packet of, in my mind, disgusting prune jam rather than the nice strawberry or raspberry jams I put on her friends' plates.

Lord, I was a jerk in those moments. And waiters like Cliff made me realize it, even if I did continue to peck through the bin for the prune jam whenever I saw her walk through the door—until one day, shoulder-pad lady finally asked me if we had any other kind of jam besides prune. The jig was up.

It took me years and a little growing up to find out why I, a pretty decent person in most other ways, would have these little spurts of meanness. I didn't know it then, but there was less time than I could have ever thought between those days of picking out packets of prune jam and potentially becoming the kind of spiteful waitress who blows cigarette smoke in the face of a nubile colleague in a break room. There were pieces of bitterness within me that might have flourished had I nurtured them.

While breakfast and lunch rushes at the Parkade Pantry were always busy, afternoons—from 2 p.m. until we closed at 4:30—were pretty slow, with the occasional store clerk or office worker coming in for a slice of pie (homemade, of course) or our famous sticky buns to savor with tea or coffee during their all-too-brief break in the day.

More than forty years later, I can still vividly see one such regular customer: a bespectacled lady with '70s-style frosted hair who seemed ancient at the time but was probably much, much younger than I am now. Every single day, she'd come in at 3:30 on the dot for hot tea and a sticky bun. And she wanted her tea just so: the hot water in one of those cute white single-serving porcelain pots we had, with two honey packets on the side.

"Don't put the tea bag in the hot water, I'll do it myself," she would say. And if anything was served other than how she ordered it, she'd politely but firmly request it be redone the way she had requested it.

"I asked you not to put the tea bag into the teapot," she'd say. "I prefer to do it myself so that the tea doesn't get too strong. Will you please make it over?"

Another day, I served the hot water for the tea directly in a cup instead of a little teapot, simply because all the porcelain pots were still in the dish room after the lunch rush.

"I prefer that the hot water be served in the teapot, as usual," she said.

Give it a rest, Frosty! I remember thinking at the time. *Lady, with all the things that are going wrong in the world, you're crabbing about getting the hot water for your tea in a cup rather than in a teapot?*

Soon I gave up and started regularly doing it the way she wanted, which is to say, the right way.

One slow afternoon, I was doing some cleaning task behind the counter while chatting with Cliff. I looked up and caught a glimpse of Miss Frosty from across the room.

There she was, in the quiet afternoon, with the sun hitting her back through the window, staring contemplatively into space and sipping tea brewed exactly the way she liked it. She simply looked so . . . happy.

In that moment, something inside me shifted.

The image of her enjoying her tea has come to me again and again over the years, and while I might not have been able to articulate why it struck me so deeply at the time, now I know: whether she had been dealing with the drudgery in some office or her own crabby clientele on the floor of one of the last remaining department stores of downtown, this was a serene moment in her day that she cherished—a moment where maybe, just maybe, things might go her way.

Perhaps I had grown up a bit. Or perhaps it was that, for the moment, standing there jawing with Cliff about this and that, and feeling a deep connectedness with those I worked with and with others who had long ago served in this great behemoth of a department store, I, too, felt happy. And part of that came from the joy of doing something well.

I must have seized on a beautiful kind of power that I never really understood I had: in spite of all the things that could go wrong in the world, I could actually do something to make someone else's world just right, if even for a moment. And it took so little to make her happy: hot water in a teapot, tea bag on the side, two packets of honey.

My last days at every other restaurant I'd worked in were uneventful, and I didn't expect things to be any different at the Parkade Pantry. After all, I only worked there for the summer. But the staff bought and signed a "goodbye and good luck" card from the sundries department next door, and Louise bought me a box of Holly Hobbie stationery (a sweet thought, but too cute to use for writing anyone except my grandmother).

More surprisingly, though, I also received a lovely plant in a flower-painted ceramic pot from two young women who were about my age but weren't headed back to college—girls with whom I had crossed paths and had a few laughs when I worked upstairs in the Tea Room now and then. I was so touched by this unexpected gift that I went to the floral department of Younkers and ordered cute little rosebud corsages for the girls to wear on their uniforms and had them sent up to the Tea Room.

Yes, department stores not only had tearooms and sundries departments but fresh floral departments, too. And college coeds needed stationery—boxes of it. And young waitresses who weren't going to college spent their hard-earned tips to buy a parting gift for another young waitress who was.

Years later, after I became a restaurant critic, when I'd encounter today's servers—those young people passing through the business, often with little ambition to stay very long—and caught glimpses of the kitchen through swinging doors, I'd wonder where the Darlenes and Tonis and Geralds and Adas and Glorias and Louises of the world had ended up. Certainly, no one was getting rich working for the Younkers restaurants, but at least the store did offer some benefits to full-time employees. Waitstaff did not have to double as janitors, as they did at Country Kitchen, and the managers did not toy with anyone about their schedules.

But equally important, our little street-level coffee shop was a tight-knit home. Indeed, if I had once thought of the Soup Kitchen as a kind of utopia, in actuality, it was the Younkers restaurants that came the closest.

Recently, I got in touch with Donna Neppl Cooper, who oversaw all of the Younkers restaurants during the years I worked there. I asked her if she remembered the way people cared for each other in the same way I did.

"We were like a small town," she said. (She'd know—she grew up in Wall Lake, Iowa, population 800.) She told me about other ways in which people cared for each other—from the top down. It was a place where a rough-and-tumble sous-chef named Buddy could become pals with a polished top Younkers executive named Stanley. And when Buddy fell in love with a waitress named Carmen, Stanley hosted the wedding and the reception in the Tea Room, inviting everyone who worked there to the afternoon celebration. And on his day off, Buddy would sometimes visit Neva, the octogenarian widow who'd worked at the Tea Room for years, and he'd do handyman work on her aging house in the faded-glory River Bend district of old Des Moines.

Donna told me of Barb, a manager in the Parkade Pantry well before my days there. When Barb became terminally ill with cancer, Younkers continued to pay her salary until she died. "They didn't think twice about doing so," said Donna. "It's simply what you did back then."

And Donna confirmed that Younkers was a place where those with challenges could find work and feel supported. She spoke of Mary, a prep cook we both fondly remembered.

"Every morning, she would pull the chicken from the bones and make homemade mayonnaise for the chicken salad," said Donna.

She mentioned others, including two table bussers who also might have had intellectual challenges, and how they had become loyal and appreciated members of the staff.

This care of employees—it pervaded everything, right down to servers at the street-level coffee shop who made sure lonely older women got extra attention and down-and-out men got enough to eat, a newspaper to read, and plenty of coffee.

Certainly, not every worker was loyal or happy. Donna spoke of servers who would go on break and then just leave. "You'd find their uniforms crumpled in the dressing room and that's the last thing you'd see of them," she said.

It's the nature of the business that people pass through, but if you stayed, there was a kind of home.

Where are those homes now? Younkers Tea Room closed when the downtown store shuttered in 2005. I often wonder where the Adas and Geralds and Marys of this world have ended up. I can only hope that there is a Toni or a Louise or a Doris who will take them under their wing day after day or a Donna or a Stanley, who, as their managers, will return their loyalty year after year.

Out of all the restaurants I've worked in, I've thought of the Parkade Pantry the most wistfully and the most often. If the Younkers restaurant was like a small town, our street-level coffee shop was its own little neighborhood in that small town, where its citizens took care of each other. Yet I remember the customers, too. Like the *Des Moines Register*'s editorial cartoonist, Frank Miller, who would walk across the street from the R&T building, sit down at the counter, and sip coffee while sketching out a later day's cartoon on the paper placemat. Or that woman who insisted on having her tea in a pot, the man who liked honey with his toast, the table of clerks who treated themselves to coffee and pie every Thursday afternoon. A group of retired men's furnishings and shoe salesmen who came in early on Saturdays, eating breakfast and then chatting around the large round table all morning long, always leaving a handsome tip—coins piled high in an unused ashtray—for keeping their coffee cups full. Though I rarely exchanged more than a dozen words a day with most of them, I still remember their faces and think of them now and then. I can still remember what they ordered. And I still feel strangely connected to all of them in some inexplicable, everlasting way.

~ 10 ~

THE PERILS OF REVIEWING RESTAURANTS

IN A MIDSIZED MIDWESTERN CITY

When it came to reviewing, my greatest joy was in finding the inauspicious-looking spot that, like Thai Flavors, ended up being a true prize; however, often what looked unpromising at first glance brought no happy surprises during the meal. A top goal in choosing a restaurant to review was newsworthiness; if an unpeopled place that looked discouraging turned out to be great, now that was worth some ink. But an unpeopled place that looked hopeless and turned out to be as dismal as it looked? That was hardly news at all.

While I was occasionally able to report on places like Thai Flavors and Bistro 43, more often there was a certain pattern to much of what I found. Again and again, I'd see big food with bulked-up sides—a pile of pasta, a huge mound of garlic mashed potatoes, an abundance of fries. Sometimes even the salads had all the heft of a bucket of lettuce. Even if I didn't personally appreciate this kind of food, I figured that if I mentioned the heft, I might send interested parties—those who sought huge portions—the restaurant's way.

Yet after a while, I started to think I wasn't doing readers any real favors by pointing them to such places. According to the Iowa Public Health Tracking Portal, a centralized resource for public health data, Iowa's rate for adult obesity in 2021 was 36.4 percent, while 34.3 percent of adults were reportedly overweight. Combined, that meant 70.7 percent of adults were either obese or overweight. I take no joy in mentioning this, but I do feel it is part of the story of our local food scene. Certainly, obesity issues are more much complicated than mere food intake—genetics, education, economic barriers, accessibility to healthy food, and physical activity can all be contributing factors. And of course, I do not wish to be insensitive to the plight of anyone who struggles with their weight. But this entrenched and pervasive trend toward huge portions in so many of our restaurants can't possibly be helping matters.

Honestly, sometimes I spent half my time annoyed at restaurateurs who habitually piled on obscene portions of food and the other half of my time being annoyed at diners who demanded they do so.

Perhaps my annoyance at restaurateurs is misplaced. Recently, Des Moines–based restaurant consultant Chris Diebel told me that when he consults on new restaurants, he tells his clients, "You can do your best to create the concept of your dreams, but ultimately, the customer decides who you are."

This leads me to believe that if big food wasn't what customers demanded, restaurants around here wouldn't serve it.

Huge portions weren't only an issue at inexpensive, belly-filling places; sometimes (though thankfully, not always) even some of our best chef-driven restaurants piled it on. I once dined with a California winemaker at a highly ambitious restaurant I had awarded five stars and which I had recommended to the group. After doing the best she could to get through a double-bone pork chop and the immense sides on her plate, this member of the California entourage set down her cutlery in frustrated surrender. "I thought this was really good when I started to eat it, but now it's just gross," she said.

A few years later, the PR firm for Comté cheese arranged a dinner for local food writers at one of our city's best restaurants. That night, I had the great pleasure of dining with a prominent award-winning California-based food writer I had long admired. Toward the end of our meal of plus-sized portions, she shook her head sadly and asked, rhetorically, about the chef's heavy-handedness. "Why did he do that to us?" she asked. What most Des Moines diners took as largesse, she took as noxious.

But what could I do? The local zeitgeist stands firmly against me on this. In our region, the food pile-on is seen as a mark of generosity. At first, I found that somewhat admirable, but later, something dawned on me: it's not like restaurateurs are giving away extra food for free. The higher they pile it on, the more you're willing to pay. And you are paying for it, in more ways than one.

In the end, I usually tried to use joy, not admonishment, to firmly nudge people toward a better experience, to make the difficult, seldom-won argument that less food can actually be better than more food.

Herb Eckhouse, founder of the Iowa-based La Quercia brand of cured meats, once told me that he judged a dining experience not only by how the food tasted while eating it but also how he *felt* after finishing the meal. I've thought often about what this means to me: After the meal, do you practically float out the door, high on fresh, vivid, thoughtfully sourced food so flavorful that you're sated with sensible portions? Or do you feel leaden and downright porcine, done in by heavy, one-dimensional food that tasted good for a few bites before becoming monotonous, before you just kept mindlessly eating to get some sense of satisfaction that the flavors alone couldn't muster? Even if the food is truly remarkable, it takes a tremendous amount of self-control to stop eating before you end up in the "Why did I do that to myself?" zone.

I tried to nudge diners toward a new kind of experience. A restaurant reviewer is not unlike an art critic. Just as abstract expressionism needed a Clement Greenberg or a Robert Hughes to help viewers appreciate what they were seeing when it burst onto the scene in the last century, sometimes my role (albeit in a much less eminent way) was to interpret a dining experience for the reader. Look, I'd say, in not so many words: this might not be what you're used to, but here's a chef who could lead you to entirely different pleasures, and together, we could all raise the standards of this city's culinary scene and help us all stop mindlessly eating so much.

Sometimes I did this by pointing out the difference between a diner's usual expectations and a new kind of experience they might enjoy if they gave it a chance. In a 2009 *Des Moines Register* review of the restaurant Proof, I wrote:

Diners in this town have become accustomed to a rather uninspired formula: Dinner begins with predictable appetizers sized to share (fried calamari, fried cheese, fried onion rings, spinach-artichoke dip, brus- chetta), followed by rote dinner salads. Then comes the entrée, followed by an oversized ooey-gooey dessert set in the middle of the table and jabbed at by everyone around the table.

This is what you call a dining rut, and if you're looking to climb out of it, book a table at Proof for their Friday night prix-fixe dinner. . . . Without having to share anything, diners enjoy a first course, second course, and to finish, either a cheese plate or dessert.

(Believe it or not, the idea of dining in discrete, smaller courses—with a first course that was not a standard lettuce salad—was still relatively rare in 2009.)

Another example comes from my review of an entirely visionary restaurant called Basil Prosperi, located in the city's East Village, a wholly off-the-beaten-path neighborhood at that time:

The mushroom bisque soup, for example, brought a thin and intensely mushroom-flavored bowl of wonder that revved up the appetite in a way that no stand-a-spoon-in-it-thick bowl of cheesy baked potato soup could ever do.

Or consider this: [A salad with] grapefruit slices showered with straw-like strips of turnip surrounded by refreshing citrus sauce. It's simple and thoughtful and does what a first course should: Suddenly, you're happy and curious and you just can't wait to see what's next. . . . Fair warning: There's no going back. Will we ever be truly happy settling into dinner with an ordinary tossed salad again?

Yes, sometimes I had to tell people that a thin soup was not a bad thing; in so many words, I was asking the diner to seize upon the intensity of the soup's flavor rather than ruing the lack of gut-busting thickness they often sought. And when did the boilerplate lettuce salad with a plop of dressing (later, the mesclun salad with a driz- zle of balsamic vinaigrette) become the standard first course in our restaurants? When restaurateurs were ready to boldly offer fresher, more creative options, I felt it was my job to point out why this shift was worth embracing.

For years, desserts rarely moved much beyond the usual options of supersized cheesecake or chocolate-goo things. When a restaurant named Alba served a pineapple carpaccio with a brittle burnt-sugar topping, crème anglaise, coconut ice cream, and delicate shavings of lime, I could hardly contain my joy. I also admired restaurateurs who knew that not having a chocolate dessert on the menu would be suicide yet tried to cajole diners into appreciating a more fascinating side of chocolate. I'm thinking of a Valrhona Napoleon served at a restaurant called Sage: strokes of mousse-like chocolate between a delicate layer of peanut crunch and paper-thin sheaths of solid chocolate.

Realistically, I knew that restaurants serving inexpensive food abundantly portioned would continue to be a mainstay in Iowa for many years to come. Yet I also hoped to garner some appreciation (and foot traffic) for those who tried to veer off the beaten path. And it was gratifying to know that my reviews could make a difference. Remembering the lovely meals at Basil Prosperi, I recently asked former co-owner Tami Johnson to tell me the impact of my review.

"Your review greatly increased our business. We became fully booked immediately with new customers," she said. She added that before my review ran, "It was so hard to get people to come to the East Village then, the location was before its time. I recall your review captured the unique energy that filled that place. . . . You put us on the map."

Tami also mentioned that she had waited on me one of the nights I visited (I always suspected a "friend" who also dined there that night had outed me). She said she had been very nervous while waiting on me. "The worry came from knowing that your reviews made a difference," she told me.

Alas, a few weeks after my review ran, my mother, playing cards at her biweekly bridge club, had to listen to her bridge partner crab about the tiny portions served in the cheese course at Basil Prosperi.

Did I really need to point out in my review that a cheese course isn't supposed to be a meal, and that if you want restaurants to serve the best artisanal cheeses, they're not going to pile them on the way they would, say, fried mozzarella sticks?

I'm happy to say that in the years since my review ran, Des Moines has embraced the artisanal cheese movement. Thanks to dedicated local purveyors who cajoled and nudged us into loving better and better products, we have more diners than ever who understand that a small slather of creamy, woodsy, and sweet Harbison soft ripened cheese from Jasper Hill Farm in Vermont is infinitely more satisfying than three or four or five times as much of a bland white supermarket cheese. But it took us years (and the hard work of indefatigable cheesemongers) to get here.

My mother having to listen to someone complain about my reviews leads me to another pitfall of being the reviewer in a midsized city: you're way too visible. You can't fade into the mass of millions of people as you can in New York or Chicago or Los Angeles. And if you lived in the city from grade school through high school and then from the age of thirty-one onward, and if you've freelanced for nearly every food editor in this major publishing hub, well, a lot of your readers know who you are.

And if they disagree with one of your reviews, they're going to tell you. And your husband, mother, and mother-in-law.

"You owe me a steak!" said a local food photographer after he visited a steakhouse that I had reviewed but that had fallen short on his visit.

"Your daughter-in-law is a pushover!" said a friend of my mother-in-law's after I gave a thumbs-up review to a restaurant she likely had a bad experience with twenty years earlier.

I once got the stink eye when I spotted an acquaintance at a great but undiscovered Vietnamese spot. I interpreted his look to be saying, "Shut your gob about this place, will ya? Let's keep it our little secret."

I'd be introduced to people at parties or out and about, and when the conversation came around to my métier, I'd get cornered for long-winded, blow-by-blow accounts of how dreadful a meal was at a place I had recommended.

Or, it was the opposite—a place I had given a tepid review was someone else's favorite place. A friend of Dave's read my review of a Vietnamese place that was fine, if nothing to drive across town for. "Man, she was way off about that place!" he said. "It's so *authentic!* When I walked through the back door, there was this faint odor of urine, and it reminded me of some of the best restaurants I dined at in Vietnam!"

How had I missed the urine-y smell—that sure mark of authenticity in a restaurant?

Of course, being known among readers means that in some cases, you'll be known among restaurateurs, too. Once you're known in one local restaurant, it won't be long before you're known in others. After a former student of Dave's worked at Bistro 43, I was outed there. Staff from there moved to other restaurants, where they outed me among an entirely new crew of servers, some of whom would invariably move on to other restaurants, and the network of knowing spiderwebbed out. I also suspect that some acquaintances, attempting to ingratiate themselves with chefs and restaurateurs, would out me if they happened to spot me at a restaurant they were dining at the same night I was.

Did I try to camouflage myself à la Ruth Reichl? In her memoir *Garlic and Sapphires*, the former *New York Times* food critic famously wrote about the great lengths she went to disguise herself when reviewing. Readers sometimes asked me if I did the same.

No, I did not. Any kind of wig or costumed getup of the sort Ruth Reichl wore would have stuck out like a sore thumb in Des Moines. The staff would've known something was up. Or, they would have said, "Good evening, Wini," and I would have felt ridiculous. I also would have had to devise disguises for Dave, and I simply did not have the time or resources to do all that.

After the third year of reviewing, I knew I'd be recognized in about 25 percent of the restaurants I went to—mainly among the chef-driven bistros, the downtown hotspots, and the newly emerging polished-casual spots. Because there was little crossover among staff between those kinds of restaurants and the many other styles of venues I reviewed, I could generally go undetected at the other 75 percent of restaurants—the ethnic spots, the suburban chains, the casual pizzerias, and the burger joints, as well as eateries in the suburbs or nearby rural Iowa.

Chris Diebel, the restaurant PR maven I mentioned earlier, who later became a restaurateur himself, once told me he had posted a photo of me above the time clocks, beverage machines, and point-of-sale terminals in all the restaurants of his clients.

I recently asked him how my being recognized might have made a difference in my experience—would they have sent out a different server? A better steak? Here's what he said:

Once you are seated, we aren't likely going to change your server. However, we may space out that server's next table to ensure they weren't in the weeds while serving a food writer. We'd tell the servers in surrounding sections that they need to be extra helpful running food because their colleague has a VIP in the section. From the back-of-house perspective, the most senior person in the kitchen (exec or sous-chef) would personally oversee plating. Ideally, that's always happening at the expo line, but leadership gets pulled in multiple directions. The front-of-house manager might step into the expo role for ten minutes while the chef focuses solely on that table.

I have no doubt that in some restaurants where I was recognized, I did get preferential treatment. What some restaurateurs didn't know (though I'm sure Chris did) was that I could almost always tell when I was recognized. And in most cases, a restaurant might have done much better had they *not* recognized me. An earlier *Des Moines Register* food critic, Josef Mossman, said it best back in 1977:

Restaurants where I am recognized humor me by pretending they don't recognize me, and the reactions follow three patterns:

(A) They fuss over me and treat me with such lavish favoritism as to incur the rancor of other diners who know what's going on. (B) They spill gravy on me. (C) They take an air of condescending hauteur as if to say, "We don't care who you are. You can't scare us."

More than twenty-five years later, my experience was almost the same. While I rarely encountered servers who were so nervous they'd spill something on me, I did get overly obsequious treatment. I remember dining at an intimate venue that was, at the time, one of our city's best restaurants; as I left, I bumped into an art director who had also been dining there that night. I asked her how her meal was. "The food was fine," she said. "But your table got all the service!" She said we had had the same waiter, who had practically ignored her party while she watched him fawn over ours.

Such fussiness—and it happened often when I was recognized—brought unease to the overall experience and generally didn't do the restaurant any favors. I could also tell I was recognized when everyone—every server in the room, every host or hostess, and any other staff member who happened to walk by the table—would stop and ask me how everything was, usually at the most inopportune times. With so many interruptions, just having a nice conversation with my tablemates became a struggle.

At the other end of the spectrum were servers who would become aloof toward our party, in that "I don't care who you are" shift Mossman described. While I didn't wish for special treatment by any means, the opposite case brought its own kind of dismay. One night, a server at a small bistro would not deign to bring me the glass of wine I had ordered to go with my entrée. She hadn't forgotten; rather, she'd glance over at me from across the room while coolly taking her time doing some other task, with a look that said, "Yes, yes, I know—you'll just have to wait." Finally, she set my glass of wine next to my near-finished plate and indifferently walked away. I'd waited tables enough in my life to know when a server is in the weeds versus sticking it to you.

In the end, how much difference did it make if I was recognized? It might have moved the needle a tad—especially at the well-staffed, on-the-ball spots for whom Diebel consulted. Yet rarely would it make a substantial difference at most other venues. Untrained servers don't suddenly become experts just because a critic shows up. Recognizing me could never make an uninspired kitchen suddenly stellar.

One night, sitting near the open kitchen at a stylish downtown venue, Dave heard the chef say to his staff, "She's here. It's quality time now." And yet, course after course proved downright dreary. *That was the best they could do?* I asked myself glumly. It was so sad, in fact, that I ended up not writing about the restaurant at all. It closed soon after.

A few nights later, I'd look forward to driving somewhere in some lesser-traveled part of town to find a place where I knew I would not be recognized, where I'd hope more than anything to find good, honest food served with genuine care by people who believed that it was always "quality time" for everyone who sat at their tables.

11

ON NASTYGRAMS

Sometime in the summer of 1980, while I was waiting tables at the Younkers Meadowlark Room in Merle Hay Mall, a thirty-something man and two young women were seated in my section just a few minutes before closing time. Because the restaurant was almost empty at this hour, the trio had my undivided attention, which is why I noticed something odd: as he walked around our extensive salad bar, the man was jotting down notes in a little oblong notebook.

After the polite but reserved party left, I conferred with the cashier. Sure enough, the name on the credit card receipt was Richard Somerville, who was at the time the *Des Moines Tribune*'s restaurant critic, then known as the "Grumpy Gourmet."

Two anxious weeks later, the review appeared in the afternoon paper. His verdict? A disappointing three out of five stars.

"Just about everything at the Meadowlark Room is classy," he wrote. "Everything, that is, except the food."

He told of a chicken cordon bleu topped with something akin to a thick yellow sauce he last saw at a well-known local greasy spoon. Bits of gristle marred the chicken crêpe filling, and the prime rib was well past the medium-rare doneness requested. He also found it unacceptable that we were out of so many things—including vanilla ice cream ("Vanilla ice cream?" he wrote).

That he deemed his server (me) "very attentive and cheerful" did little to assuage how flattened we all were by his review. The sous-chef who'd overseen the kitchen the night of the critic's visit—usually one proud, swaggering dude—could hardly look the rest of us in the eye.

We all knew we were a better restaurant than the one Somerville visited that night, and I decided to tell him so. On my day off, I sat down to write a letter to the *Tribune* that told him just how off the mark his review was.

But as I began to draft the letter, I realized I didn't have much of an argument. Everything he said was true. The prime rib was overdone. We were out of a ridiculous number of things (the sous-chef in charge of ordering had made some major errors). While that wee bit of gristle in the crêpe attested to the way the chicken was cooked fresh and plucked from the bone every single day, it was still a flaw. And why were we serving such a prefab chicken gravy on the cordon bleu when so much of everything else we served was made from scratch?

I never did finish that letter.

About the only error of fact Somerville did make was that he mentioned he had arrived around thirty minutes before closing, when in fact, he had been seated just minutes before we closed. Yet I knew his error was irrelevant. His near-closing-time arrival was absolutely no excuse for a subpar experience—every restaurant I had ever worked in taught me so.

Mr. Somerville could only base his review on the meal he was served. Though it broke our hearts, his reporting on the food was pretty much unassailable. The kitchen immediately went to work to address the issues he had raised. And yes, it hurt, but we became a better restaurant for it. I doubt we ever ran out of vanilla ice cream again.

During my years as the Datebook Diner, the paper would often receive letters from readers and restaurateurs who disagreed with my reviews. My editors called them "nastygrams." From the beginning, I knew I wanted my reviews to be as fair and accurate as an opinionated critique can be. I highlighted the best things about a place, even if, in consideration of readers who trusted me, I pointed out what I perceived as the downsides, too.

I tried to write in a way that, if someone did sit down to write a letter that took issue with my review, as they read each flaw I had pointed out, they wouldn't think, *How dare she*, but rather, *Well, she has a point there*.

Some of the mail we received was from loyal customers of a restaurant I had found lacking in some way. It may sound counterintuitive, but I loved it when the *Register* would print these letters. In the days before everyone became a restaurant critic (i.e., the days before crowdsourced review sites like Yelp), the power I had as the paper's chief restaurant critic weighed heavily on me. If someone was happy to put their good name out there and vouch for a restaurant I had found subpar, it made my power less of a burden.

I also got letters from restaurateurs, but rather than disputing specific points I made in the reviews, they'd sometimes be more general, accusing me of, for example, "not supporting local businesses" when I pointed out flaws. I never saw my job as being a cheerleader for local businesses per se. While nothing about reviewing ever made me happier than reporting on a great local venue, my loyalty would always be to the reader. These letters, however, were generally thoughtfully and respectfully written.

Both diners and restaurateurs would sometimes say I was biased, but they never said what they thought I was biased toward. Good food? Expert service?

I had been warned that other types of letters might make their way to me. Reviewers before me had received *true* nastygrams: I'd been told that someone threatened to kill one previous reviewer's horse (how *Godfather*-esque!). When the same reviewer mentioned finding gristle in a pork tenderloin sandwich at a restaurant, the restaurateur wrote that "the only gristle at their restaurant was in [the reviewer's] thighs."

When I did receive a threatening letter telling me, among other things, that they knew where I lived and that "I'd better watch my back," my editor told me I should mention it to the police, just in case. A policeman came to visit me at my home, read the letter, shook his head, and said, "These people. They just have to get something off their chests, and then they're over it. You won't hear from this person again."

The officer was right, or almost. I did not hear from that particular poison-pen writer until many years later. After I quit reviewing restaurants but still wrote for the *Register*, my photo appeared in the paper. The angle made it look like my breasts were much larger than they actually are.

I received a letter in the same distinctive handwriting as the threatening letter fourteen years prior. The correspondent wrote: "Wow, you must have paid a fortune for that boob job! Too bad you're still *butt ugly*."

I can't tell you how much that letter did *not* bother me. In fact, as I write this, I'm chuckling out loud at the absurdity of it.

There were, however, letters that were much harder to get over. Like this one:

> I recently ate at the restaurant Bistro 43 because in your review of it you had given it a five-star rating, the highest you could give. The night I dined there, I would have been hard pressed to give the food, service, or ambiance anything rated above a two. What a disappointment to leave a restaurant hungry and feeling you've been misled.

That, dear reader, bothered me more than is probably sane. The thought that a reader felt I had misled them was unbearable to me. I quickly learned it was important to be as scrupulous in my accolades as I was in my criticisms. Throwing around compliments is the easiest thing in the world to do, but I had to remember that overzealousness could lead to disappointments—disappointments endured by people who had trusted me to guide them where to spend their hard-earned money and hard-won leisure time.

I still stand by the five stars I gave Bistro 43. It was an extraordinary restaurant in every way. But if I were to write the review again, I would have been even more clear about the kind of place it was. Des Moines diners weren't used to five-star restaurants that served less familiar food in unassuming neighborhood spots. I should have said something like, "If you're looking for steak Diane in a hushed formal dining room complete with crystal chandeliers and tuxedoed maître d's, this isn't your place. Instead, come here to experience a new kind of five-star experience—and all the joys that can come from a buzzy chef-driven restaurant housed in a handsomely renovated former Maid-Rite."

It was important not only to tell people why they might also enjoy a place I loved but perhaps also key them into why it might not be their kind of place at all.

Other letters and emails came from grammar tyrants, those who would quibble with errors I had made (and that had on rare occasion slipped through the copyeditors). I once wrote that something made me "feel badly." Oops. Correct usage is "feel bad." One email told me there was no such thing as "walleye pike." It was either walleye or pike. He said I should have grilled the server about which it was. He was wrong, but it took me an inordinate amount of time to chase that factoid down in the early days of the internet.

Then there was the reader who rightly quibbled with my use of the term "au jus" when I wrote something like "the side of au jus was generous and savory." Au jus is not a noun; rather, it's a prepositional phrase, meaning "with jus" (i.e., served with the meat juices). I should have simply referred to the meat juices as "jus."

"I'd expect a restaurant critic to know this," the reader wrote.

Ouch. That one hurt. Indeed, she was right. It was a rookie mistake on my part. And the sad thing was, I did know this.

Oh, how I knew this . . .

～12～

AU JUS RHYMES WITH . . .

If you ever have to work in a joyless workplace, I hope for your sake there will in any case be a kind of solidarity between yourself and others in the organization. At least you can commiserate and maybe even find a little humor now and then in the situation. Sadly, such a vibe was far from present at the private dining club I worked for after college.

After the suburban Younkers was rebuilt after the fire, it reopened in the autumn of 1979. I worked at its Meadowlark restaurant throughout college full time during the summers, plus now and then on semester breaks, holiday weekends—whenever I wanted, really. Gladys had retired, but I could call up Wilma any weekend I was coming into town and ask for a shift or two. Business at the Meadowlark was going gangbusters, so she was always glad to have me.

The new department-store restaurant had taken a few giant leaps into the fine-dining realm. We now had a bar that served limited cocktails, beer, and wine. Booths with indigo leather seats and decorative tile ran along two sides of the room; two-tops with banquette seating lined another side. Curved banquettes with oval tables surrounded the etched-glass enclosed salad bar gazebo, and the rest of the room was furnished with handsome, high-quality mahogany tables and chairs. Coffee was poured from shiny silver-esque pots, and water was brought to the table in honest-to-God crystal. Gone were the paper placemats; each table was draped in almost elegant faux-jacquard linen. A prime rib dinner, complete with the salad bar, cost around six dollars—the price had climbed over the five years I had worked for Younkers, but it was still a steal.

Tips started growing more frequent and more substantial; we were thrilled to see less loose change and more paper money. I'll never forget the first time I saw a five-dollar bill left on the table for a party of four. Today's 20 percent standard was a long way off—10 percent was still a good tip. But because more people were tipping than ever before, I made more money than I'd ever made in my life.

With the funds I had saved in high school and what I made from the Meadowlark during college, I was able to nab a BA not only debt free but with about a grand in the bank. In 1980, tuition at the University of Iowa was $475 a semester; my rent was $110 a month. Throw in a couple hundred dollars a month for food and beer, and each academic year from 1978 to 1982 cost me about $2,500.

No wonder I felt the freedom to be a French and English major. I loved France and I loved literature. I wasn't racking up any kind of debt, so I had the luxury to study exactly what I wanted and could worry about the details—like a career and such—later. What a gift, to spend four years learning about everything from terminal moraines to ancient religions of the East, memorizing Shakespeare couplets for a quiz, studying French romantics like François-René de Chateaubriand, who made me see how even the most tender stems of this year's weeds pierce their way through the oldest and toughest stone fortifications. I envisioned myself as one of those tender green shoots—not sure where or which way I would grow, but hopeful that I would somehow flourish in my own way.

But such fanciful thinking, along with my stretch of historical-economic great luck, came to a crash-bang halt when I graduated from college in 1982. The 1981 through 1982 recession was in full swing. Unemployment reached 10.8 percent—the highest it had been since 1940.

Funny thing was, while I knew we were in a recession, I didn't know how bad unemployment was until many years later. I figured my inability to find decent work was a result of personal failure, bad planning on my part. But even friends who majored in business were thankful to have jobs at department-store cosmetic counters and bank branch reception desks. My BA in French and English with no experience stood no chance in Des Moines. I knew that to get a nonretail, nonrestaurant job, I would have to move somewhere else in the world.

But first, I needed money. And about the only thing I knew how to do well was wait tables.

Sadly, by 1982, the Meadowlark's star had started to fade. While Des Moines still remained mostly a steak-and-spaghetti stronghold, a handful of the newer restaurants that came to town had started serving things like champagne brunch and gourmet burgers; one spot even had duck flambéed tableside. We also started seeing a small number of new (to our neck of the woods) possibilities ranging from Szechuan Chinese to increasingly good Mexican food. Against those options, the Meadowlark was starting to look a little fuddy-duddy.

Plus, with the recession in full swing, lunch out was a once-in-a-while treat. Even sold at a loss, our prime rib dinner was now a splurge for those being squeezed out of the middle class. And if you were going to go spendy on a rare night out, the tug of the new was hard to resist.

Customers no longer had to wait in line for a table. On slow nights, my colleagues and I would sometimes find ourselves standing alongside a server's station, hungrily watching the hostess lead a party to a table, hoping they'd be seated in our section. For the possibility of making a tip. For something to do.

Gone were the tables draped in linens; to save money, we'd gone back to using placemats. Options on the salad bar were scaled back. We had started serving quiches and cheesecakes that simply weren't to the level of what we'd served in the past; I'm pretty sure that, to cut corners, the kitchen had started serving a few things that came in on a food-service truck versus being homemade in the downtown Tea Room kitchen.

By this time, Wilma had retired and the new management was not as generous with the hours. I had become a part-time on-call employee, given a shift now and then—mostly Thursday and Friday nights and weekend lunches.

An older coworker, whom I'd gotten along with quite well for the previous couple years, pointed out something I pretty much knew but no one had actually said aloud: whenever I got a shift, it meant there was another server on the floor, and everyone else had fewer tables. Which meant everyone went home with fewer tips.

"I need this money to feed my girls," Kathy said with more melancholy than bitterness. "I'm not just taking my tips through the mall and buying candy at Fannie Farmer and frilly new tops at Paul Harris on my way to my car."

I wasn't either, but I understood her resentment.

Clearly, working twelve hours a week in a slow restaurant was getting me nowhere. I needed a new job. A great friend of mine who was attending the local business college by day was working in a private club at night.

"You're lucky," Jeanine said. "College graduates usually get to start in the formal dining room. Others have to start in banquets and work their way up." She was right. In light of my degree, my longtime restaurant experience, and a good recommendation from Younkers, I was given a coveted position in the formal dining room, starting at $6.40 an hour rather than what the banquet servers were paid (something like $5.90). What luck.

Though waiting tables wasn't my ultimate aspiration, I was glad to be moving up in the profession. At that time, private clubs were among the very best restaurants in town. At least I'd made the leap into fine dining. And yet, I soon found there was something diminishing about waitressing at the private club—more so than at any other restaurant (besides Country Kitchen) that had ever employed me.

My disappointment started with the employee meal. Certainly I understood that the meal wouldn't be steak, shrimp, and other stripes of high-end food served in the formal dining room, but I figured it would at least be good. And surely I looked forward to the preshift camaraderie, which had been key, especially at Younkers and Baker's. At Baker's the preshift meal was one of the best things about working there. In the later days of working at the Meadowlark, those who worked the full day—both lunch and dinner shifts—would often have to wait until midafternoon to take their breaks, two or three servers at a time, staggered throughout the slow hours. It was usually a good time. Without the opportunity for all of us to sit down together at once, some of us would often gather in the dining room about a half hour before work in the mornings just to drink coffee and gab before we clocked in. We enjoyed each other's company.

But in the case of the employee meals at the club, there was very little that was familial about our meals together. The food and time we spent eating it brought little connection, cheer, or sense of well-being to my work.

With the exception of Country Kitchen, at other restaurants I'd worked in, we always ate our meals somewhere in the dining room, whether in the little party nook at Baker's, at the end of the busy counter at the Parkade Pantry, or at a cloth-draped table in the far corner of the vast Meadowlark Room.

At the club we sat at a large bare table in a cramped and windowless break room, where the cinder-block walls were painted an industrial yellow and the focal point was the time clock flanked by two racks of timecards. Nearby, a service elevator clanged, and the dishwashers splashed and gurgled and smelled of detergent and old food. We could sit down any time after 4:30 and had to clock in at 5:00 to ready the dining room, server stations, and all else before guests arrived. Most reservations began at 6:00, but it was a club: if a member wanted or needed to dine earlier, we'd accommodate them. It was not uncommon for guests to arrive at 5:30 for predinner cocktails. We had to be ready.

So there we sat, a rotating shift of us quickly gulping down our meals, some smoking cigarettes and putting them out on the detritus of their plates before scraping the remains into the trash can of the nearby dishwashing operations, and clocking in.

The club was the only place I'd ever worked where the food the employees ate was thoroughly different from what the guests ate. The Soup Kitchen and the Meadowlark fed us for free; Country Kitchen and Baker's Cafeteria charged us half price for what we ate. In all cases, we could eat whatever was on the menu except for a few select things (prime rib, expensive seafood platters).

The club fed us for free, so there was that. Yet while they didn't let us go hungry, they left us hungering for something else.

Our dinners had all the finesse of leftovers from previous banquets or lunch service or things cobbled together, I suspect, from whatever foods might be nearing an expiration date. Some days might see warmed-over French toast and breakfast meats salvaged from a previous breakfast service. The day after a buffet-style banquet, we might get some rigatoni and a few scant meatballs, the tomato sauce pasty and dry from the reheat. Dinosaur bones—beef ribs cut from prime rib baked in barbecue sauce—were a recurring specialty. They sounded promising but had been trimmed so close they were mostly bone and sauce. Chicken salad that was likely in danger of expiring would be topped with breadcrumbs and baked, then plopped into a steam tray and served as some sort of glum chicken casserole.

I remember once, when there were no leftovers to be had, the sous-chef in charge of the meal made a fresh pan of moist, fluffy, beautifully scrambled eggs, crisp bacon, biscuits, and some chicken gravy he whipped up minutes before our mealtime. He had prepped cantaloupe and honeydew melon (into graceful balls, no less), added some blueberries, and splashed it all with a little kirsch. It was simple but it was fresh, and it was heaven compared to the slop we normally ate. That was one of the few good meals I remember eating during my year and a half at the club. With such talent in the kitchen, I often wondered why we couldn't dine like this—inexpensively but well—more often.

Looking back, I also wonder why we couldn't have dined in a more pleasant corner of the club: a banquet room not in use, with large windows overlooking the changing seasons. But that was before I knew, or expected, anything better.

Back then, employee meals were simply not a priority. To this day, I don't know if management did not consider how good, thoughtful food could bring a little joy to the night and camaraderie to the team, or if they simply didn't care. When thinking back to our meals, I think of an oft-cited quote from Virginia Woolf: "One cannot think well, love well, sleep well, if one has not dined well."

Because restaurant work demands a certain kind of love, I would add that one cannot wait tables well if one has not dined well, either.

At the club, servers were compensated differently from other places where I had waited tables. To every check, a 15 percent service charge was automatically added. At the time 15 percent was the upper level of the tipping spectrum. I often suspected that many club members assumed the service charge went directly to their server, so understandably, they never felt the need to tip on top of that.

The truth, however, was that I never directly saw any of the service charge. On any given night, I made $6.40 an hour whether I waited on twenty people or fifty. That's because traditionally, many country clubs and private dining clubs have used such service charges to pad the club's overall bottom line. In the best cases, the revenue from the 15 percent upcharge is used to pay higher wages across the entire workforce.

At the club, the system seemed to work well enough. I don't know what the line and prep cooks were paid, but I'm pretty sure the wage disparity between the servers and nonmanagerial kitchen staff was not as high as it is in many restaurants today.

It also meant that I didn't dread slow nights—I'd make as much per hour on a slow Tuesday night as on a frantically busy Saturday. For the members, it meant they didn't have to make a judgment call every time the bill was presented (10 percent? 12 percent? 15 percent?). And because servers got no more compensation when a party ordered our house Inglenook wine by the glass instead of our highest-end bottle, nobody was trying to upsell anything.

The downside? While the system was better for the kitchen staff, in all honesty, I missed the excitement and motivation of working for tips. In past waitressing jobs, checking out the tip brought a certain suspense and that gratifying *ka-ching* after each table left. I also wasn't used to waiting two weeks for a paycheck to have money in my pocket.

And, frankly—I don't even know how to say this without exposing a major chink in my mighty (albeit self-reported) work-ethic armor—but without the incentive of a tip that was left to the diner's discretion, I'm not really sure I was the club's best server.

Certainly, I did everything by the book exactly as I was told. I was generally courteous and professional to the members. In fact, I truly enjoyed learning the ins and outs of fine-dining service. Training for formal dining service took an entire week (instead of a few hours, which was the case in every other restaurant I'd worked). Dining at the club was wrought with a rigor and style that I'd never experienced when dining out, much less effected as a server myself.

Water glasses were filled and cocktails offered within seconds after guests were seated. After the cocktails were placed, the menus were presented either by the section's captain or the maître d'. Later, the server would take the food order, always starting with the ladies, followed by the member's guests. The captain would arrive to discuss the wine order and subsequently present and serve the wine.

Courses were served in precisely timed fashion, and we kept eagle eyes on our tables to make sure each course's plates and used silverware were cleared as soon as (but not a second before) the last guest had finished the course. Many of our dishes—Caesar salad, hot spinach salad, flambéed shrimp, steak Diane, Chateaubriand with a bouquetière of vegetables, bananas Foster—were prepared and often flambéed tableside by the captain as the servers stood by, linen service cloths draped over our forearms, ready to present the handsomely plated food. Water glasses were continually kept full by the bus staff (who otherwise did not interact directly with guests). Everything—every glass, plate, spoon, ramekin—was always, without exception, presented from a tray. Changing linens on the table required two servers: one to unfold the new cloth across the table while the other rolled the used cloth away, thus never leaving any part of the inelegantly bare table exposed.

While part of me inwardly rolled my eyes at some of the fussiness, I appreciated the intricacy of the dance. There was a grace and artistry to the motions that kept them from getting boring. And I did feel rather proud of myself after perfecting the finer points, such as the tabletop technique of skillfully slicing, opening, and folding back the parchment paper for the snapper baked en papillote, or the one-handed method of using a serving fork and spoon (rather than using workaday tongs) to serve vegetables tableside from a hot pan. Now and again, I could feel that my work required grace, expertise, and know-how, that there was some true dignity in the work we all did at the club.

And yet, I never felt that management afforded much respect for our profession. We were rarely complimented on our work. Our dining room manager confided that when he had written up his staff's yearly evaluations, he had been told to curb his praises a notch. Perhaps the über-managers didn't want us thinking we were all that (nor, I suspect, did they want us to expect the better raises that usually come with glowing reviews).

We were reminded daily of our inadequacy via dopey motivational posters that management had framed in a glass case right by the employee entrance. They were the first thing we saw as we walked through door for work and the last thing we saw as we left.

The posters must have been part of some kind of subscription service because they changed weekly. Each featured a colorful cartoon of squat, goofy-looking, big-shoed children in cutesy situations, with some kind of workplace platitude printed alongside. I recently found some of these on the internet, and yes, they were as dumb as I remember them. A few examples . . .

One shows a boy walking away from a stream with a fishing pole, frowning, dejected and fishless, while his ecstatic buddy pulls a big one out of the water. The slogan reminds employees not to quit until the work is done.

Another shows a boy sitting on the grounded end of a seesaw plank, with the up-in-the-air end bereft of the partner that makes the game work. The slogan admonishes us to avoid absenteeism, because everyone will miss you if you're out.

Yet another depicts three children pulling on a rope as if on the winning side of a tug-of-war. This one is, of course, about the winning results of teamwork.

These posters taught basic workplace courtesies in the most dumbed-down ways, hinting to the staff that not only did we not know how to act, but we weren't very bright, either.

It's hard to imagine that no one else found the posters condescending, but not one of my coworkers ever said a word about them. The club was simply not the kind of place you'd share your musings and doubts with others.

There was a kind of hierarchy among the staff. In the front of the house, the formally trained servers were at the top of the heap, though bartenders thought they were alongside the top dogs. Cocktail servers and grill servers were midstatus, while banquet servers occupied the lower echelon. Those on the upper rungs of the bartending and waitstaff were often surprisingly bossy toward those on the lower rungs, even though none were in management.

Most of the formal dining room servers had been to college, and sometimes among the rest of the staff, there was an undercurrent of disdain for anyone who had a degree. The attitude was, "If you're so smart, how come you're waiting tables?"

The thing is, few of us thought we were really that smart. Indeed, because we had gone to college, we were hyperaware of how much we *didn't* know. But we were hardly going to get any points for that wise little nugget.

In fact, sometimes it was best to hide anything you did know—as was the case with the French term "au jus."

I knew that literally "au jus" meant "with juice," and the term referred to meats served with their cooking juices. At every restaurant I'd ever worked at in Iowa, everyone used the term "au jus" to refer to the little bowl of juice itself, which was technically wrong (the stuff in the bowl is juice, not *with* juice.) Everyone also pronounced it "AWE juice" rather than the French way, "oh ZSHEW."

This, I could live with. We were in Iowa, after all. Certainly, we don't say "pair-EE" when we mean Paris, do we?

But then one night, going with the flow, I asked for an extra bowl of "AWE juice." A cook, who must have just recently learned how to pronounce it, corrected me.

"Jesus. I thought you knew French. It's 'oh ZSHEW'," he admonished. "Oh ZSHEW, Wini. Oh ZSHEW. Oh ZSHEW. Oh ZSHEW."

A server, who happened to be standing nearby, said. "Got it, Derek. Easy to remember: 'au jus' rhymes with 'F-U.'"

Clearly, this wasn't the time to mention that there should be no "au" about it. Nor that "au jus" and "F-U" were more of a slant rhyme than a perfect rhyme. I got my bowl of greasy meat juice and quietly got the hell out of the kitchen.

Years after I had worked at the club, I ran into a former bartender I had worked with there. I mentioned that I recognized her from our club days. "Yes. You were probably one of those waitresses I terrorized," she said, with an apology in her voice. (Terrorized was a bit strong, but certainly, she was never kind. Snarky? Yes.)

What was it about the place that made colleagues work against each other so? Perhaps it was a combination of everything: the bad meals, those motivational posters, the knowing that there was 10.8 percent unemployment and we were all stuck here for a while. The club was also the only place I'd ever worked where there was such a great social divide between those who served and those who dined. Everywhere else I'd worked was a place where the staff could have afforded to eat at once in a while if they wanted to. The pleasures of the club were profoundly out of our reach. We could smell but could never savor the food we served. I can't help but think that this added a certain kind of resentment.

With a collective understanding of our powerlessness, trivial matters often took on an outsize importance. Minibattles could erupt over the smallest things. Though the stakes were low, at most every turn, the bitterness, it seemed, was sky high.

So, what were the members themselves like? It's strange. I can still remember the faces of some customers at the restaurants of my earlier youth: the little boy and his pecan pie at Country Kitchen, the old coot who once held fast to my plump fifteen-year-old hand at Baker's Cafeteria, Miss Frosty and her perfect cup of tea at the Parkade Pantry, plus many, many others. Their faces will come to me sometimes, triggered by something as fleeting as the sound of dishes being stacked or the smells of beefy restaurant food mingling with tabletop cleansers.

But I can hardly remember any faces of the members at the club, even though I waited on them six days a week for one-and-a-half years (an eternity when you're twenty-two to twenty-three).

Certainly, the haute bourgeoisie was nothing to get worked up against, as some of my college critical-theory literature texts had led me to believe. Rather, the private-club crowd was like any other group I'd crossed paths with. Some were perfectly nice; these were the people who would look me in the eye and say "thank you" now and then. Or maybe even ask how I was after I had asked them the same. Others were not so nice; they'd never glance up from their menu when ordering or say anything to me that wasn't some kind of command. Most, however, were in between decent. The real trouble was this: amid serving them all those flambéed shrimp and steak Dianes, Smith and Kearns and gin martinis, I felt no connection to them at all. And the feeling, I'm sure, was mutual.

During this low stretch of my life, I was living at home with my parents, who constantly wondered (very much aloud) why I wasn't doing something better with my life. I did, after all, have a college degree. While Mom had had a brief secretarial-school stint, neither had never been to college, so they took it quite hard that I was waiting tables and living at home.

"I'm only twenty-two!" I tried to reason with them once. "What, exactly, were *you* doing when you were twenty-two that was so great?"

"I was in the service," said my dad, which was his modest way of saying that he was on the front lines fighting Nazis from North Africa to Italy.

"Managing the downtown bus depot, because all the men who normally managed the bus depot had gone off to the service," said my mom.

This by no means helped me feel better about having a low-paying, joyless job. It also made me feel pretty darned foolish for feeling sorry for myself for having such a low-paying, joyless—and pretty unheroic—job.

Sounding a little bit like the guy in *The Graduate* who tells Benjamin Braddock he needs to get into "plastics," my mom kept telling me I should "get into computers," though I'm sure she had little idea what that really meant (Software? Hardware? Coding?). She also thought I needed to become a better typist. She got out her manuals from her 1930s-era high school typing classes, set up her manual typewriter on the dining room table, and cajoled me into brushing up on the skill.

About a year later, after passing a typing test at an employment agency in New York and scoring my first nonretail, nonwaitressing job there, I was forever grateful to my mother for making me do this. But in 1982, I spit nails every time I sat down to the keyboard to type "Now is the time for all good men to come to the aid of their country" and other insipid drills.

My goal was to "get into publishing," though, like Mom and her "computers," I only had a vague idea as to what that actually meant.

America loves its stories of self-made success—people who go from, for example, toiling away at a dispiriting $6.40-an-hour waitressing job at a private club to becoming a wine writer who gets flown across the world to sample wines at their source. It's a good yarn, and while getting someplace better than you are might take talent, hard work, and moxie, never, ever underestimate the great randomness of where you fall in whatever industry in which you wish to prevail.

Magazine publishing was accelerating—the 1970s and 1980s saw a proliferation of niche publications, from *Country Living* and *Working Mother*, to *Self* and *Skydiving*, to *Guitar World* and *Wine Spectator*.

Publishers hired recent college grads to type, file, and answer the phone—jobs that had titles such as editorial assistant, publicity assistant, and marketing assistant but were purely secretarial in nature. These were the days before desktop publishing, when manuscripts, magazines, book catalogs, and sales materials were still typed on rudimentary word processors and sent to typesetters and then to designers working at pasteup boards to be made into mechanicals and sent off for printing.

It took a lot of low-level people to get books, magazines, and catalogs out there, and while the jobs were patently unglamorous, it's how nearly everyone I knew (save those with deep East Coast industry connections) got their foot in the door of a publishing house. The unstated contract was that most newcomers would be promoted to the next level after about a year of paying your dues. Soon, you might be doing some actual wordsmithing, perhaps a little proofreading, copyediting, or fact checking, maybe even a little writing here and there, or at least writing catalog copy and press releases.

I knew I needed to move someplace where my BA in French and English might get me through a door, as it wasn't happening in Des Moines. After the recession ended in late 1982, the doors to the publishing world were once again wide open to entry-level twenty-somethings like me. Dozens of jobs appeared in the *New York Times* each week. Dave (my future husband) and I set our sights on heading that way, eventually landing a job that opened the door to everything else I ever did.

But first, we had promised ourselves a post-college backpacking trip through Europe. Dave was making $3.60 an hour working as an inventory clerk at his brother's art supply store; he, too, was living with his parents. By working split shifts on Tuesdays through Fridays, plus Saturday nights and Sunday dinners, I worked forty hours and took home about $175 a week. My parents charged me nominal rent—to teach me some kind of lesson about there being no free lunches or something like that—plus I had to pay the upkeep on our family's aging Buick Opel, which chewed up one month's salary when it needed some major repair. After expenses, it took me about eight months to earn enough for a two-month trip plus a jump start on funds for a possible move elsewhere in the world once we returned home.

We left for Europe in mid-March, armed with a copy of Arthur Frommer's *Europe on $20 a Day*, a two-month Eurail pass, a ten-day BritRail pass, and about $1,600 each in traveler's checks in Dutch guilders, French francs, German marks, British pounds, and U.S. dollars.

We arrived in Amsterdam, and for the first two weeks of the trip, we duly went to all the art museums and cathedrals and sites that pretty much all backpackers went to. We saw Rembrandts and Vermeers in the Rijksmuseum, van Goghs and Toulouse-Lautrecs in the Van Gogh Museum; we were awed by the Cologne Cathedral. We wandered through the Alte Pinakothek and the Neue Pinakothek in Munich, too many museums in Florence, the antiquities in Rome, and then suddenly we were done with sites and museums and art that was mildly interesting but seemed to only pass the time, time that we knew would soon run out. Besides, we knew the show was elsewhere.

By the third week of the trip, we preferred sitting in cafés and parks, watching cats unsuccessfully chase pigeons or children kick soccer balls that flew too close to a bench of crabby old ladies who spit out words we didn't know but pretty much understood; we liked seeing high school girls smoking cigarettes and keeping a cool eye on the nearby boys while flaunting their ripeness reminiscent of Beatrice and Dante in a postcard we saw all over Florence. We liked drinking wine and eating cheese and fruit and bread with mortadella or prosciutto or pâté in our little compartments on the train as hill towns and vineyards and mustard fields sped by. We liked sitting on benches by lakes and beaches and walking hilly trails and ambling through gritty neighborhoods and dusty small towns with ruins and wondering what we would find around the next corner. We loved not knowing.

We loved the cheap food—weisswurst mit brot, a sausage served with a pretzel in Munich; a filling goulash soup served with fresh white bread and butter in Salzburg; crisp-skinned roast chicken with France's magical crispy-puffy frites in Paris. Arthur Frommer advised us to nab some leberkäse ("I'm dreaming of it now!" he wrote convincingly) the minute we got off the train at the station in Munich, and so we did. The specialty resembled thick-cut bologna with a vague liver-like taste; in truth, it wasn't really all that. Yet stopping to celebrate our arrival in Munich, enjoying a little snack with a big beer amid the hustle and rush of the Hauptbahnhof, was just what we needed after a long train ride in sweaty second class, feeling increasingly grimy at every stop.

In Venice, spaghetti alle vongole—spaghetti with tiny clams in the shell, parsley, and more garlic than I'd ever seen in one place—tasted like nothing I'd ever had in my life and helped clear my head from a bad spring cold. Crisp and lemony veal Milanese in Florence, our first-ever truly thin-crust pizza in Rome, pissaladière in the south of France. While we could only afford a cheap version of bouillabaisse (with fish but no high-end shellfish) in Nice, the exotic perfume of the soup combined with the welcome heft of the meaty fish—for $7.50— was a hungry backpacker's dream.

Again and again what struck me, and made me happy and sad at the same time, was that no matter how humble the place we frequented, and no matter how unfashionable we looked (sturdy hiking shoes, wool socks, pilling sweaters) or how poorly we pronounced the basic words from our phrase books, we were usually served with a level of care and attention that made us feel we had chosen well, that we were—at that very moment—exactly where we were supposed to be in the world.

A white-jacketed waiter at an unassuming trattoria near the train station in Venice forgot to bring us aperitivos we had ordered to start our meal. After ten minutes passed, I turned from our table on the terrace and spotted him standing in the doorway. He caught my eye and suddenly remembered. He rushed into the restaurant and then rushed back out with our little ninety-cent martini biancos.

"Sorry!" he said—likely one of a handful of English words he spoke. He seemed truly crushed that he had made us wait longer than we should have to experience those first few sips of well-being.

In Munich at the über-touristy Hofbräuhaus, as we settled our bill, we noticed that the older Frau accidentally overcharged us for two more beers than we had drunk. When we brought it to her attention (in bad phrase-book German), she quickly corrected the error and apologized in abundance.

"Das ist . . . no problem," I said, trying to make her feel better but not quite having the words to do so.

"Das ist NICHT 'no problem!'" she answered. She seemed embarrassed and even a little ashamed, as if we might think she was trying to take advantage of us.

In Spain, grabbing a beer at a workaday bar-restaurant near the train station of a city we stopped in during a brief layover, we were handed a plate of pescaditos fritos, those crispy floured-and-fried minnow-sized fish. I looked at them warily, not sure if you were supposed to eat the whole things. Noting my reluctance, the bartender picked one up by the tail and ate it, head, bones, and all except for the tip of the tail. We followed suit and happily cleared our plate.

A little while later, he came out from the kitchen with a twelve-inch head-on, tail-on fish in his hands, wordlessly but unmistakably joking that we were to eat it head, bones, and all, too. It was a touching bit of clowning around that happened without any of us speaking more than two or three words of each other's language.

Of course, not every single person we encountered across two months of dining in European restaurants was kind. Among our few rude encounters was a waitress in Avignon at a casual sidewalk restaurant. As she cleared away our first course (a fine little pâté), she asked us if we had enjoyed it. I told her it was "delicieux." Of course, I pronounced this mostly wrong (dee-lish-ee-yuh).

"Duh-lee-see-yuh," she corrected me, saying each syllable slowly as if I were dim-witted rather than simply someone who had learned French outside of France. Occasionally through the rest of our meal, I heard her imitating my bad pronunciation with her coworkers. If such a thing had been the norm throughout the trip, I might have gotten used to it. But that night, it was a rare and puzzling outlier to most everything else I had experienced; I just could not shake it. I can't tell you what else we ate for dinner, but I can still hear her mockingly saying "Deelisheeyuh! Deelisheeyuh! Deelisheeyuh!"

But Avignon will always have a place in my heart, as it was there that, in the midst of thinking about what a soul-crushing place the club truly was, I realized it didn't have to be that way.

We got into Avignon late in the day. After finding a cheap hotel recommended in our guidebook, we set out to menu-shop for dinner. We knew it was likely too early to be seated, but we were hungry, as we had only had bread and cheese and fruit on the train much earlier in the day.

As we walked past a courtyard behind a restaurant hidden by trellises and vines and a ceiling of flowering plants, we heard the unmistakable sounds of people enjoying a good meal on the terrace: the hushed roll of conversation and the occasional laughter against the clattering of silverware against plates. *Aha*, we thought, *here's a place that's open.*

We stepped into the courtyard and saw a group of restaurant workers—cooks in their whites, servers in their black trousers or skirts and white shirts or blouses, a maître-d' with his black jacket draped over the chair. They were sitting around a table, enjoying a meal together. I saw wineglasses and carafes of both water and wine and large empty pots of food and platters of mostly eaten cheese on the paper-topped, cloth-draped tables that had been jammed together for the small gathering. Just as I walked in, a woman in a floral dress—likely the proprietress—came out with a tray full of little cups of espresso with little cubes of sugar and little teaspoons and began to serve everyone; some at the table began lighting their after-dinner cigarettes.

I knew immediately that we had walked in on the employee meal, and it would be some time before the restaurant opened.

"Bonsoir, monsieur, mademoiselle," the woman in the floral dress called over to us, a bit quizzically.

"Bonsoir, madame. Le restaurant n'est pas ouverte?" The restaurant is not open? I managed to ask, stating the obvious in the way one often does in a second language when more subtle phrases prove elusive.

"Vers dix-neuf heures et demie," she answered, apologetic but firm, telling me that the restaurant would open around 7:30.

I said merci and somewhat sheepishly began to walk away. How silly of me to think a nice restaurant like that would be open any sooner.

But then a very sweet thing happened. From the table, an older cook—the chef perhaps— gesturing with a cigarette in hand, shouted, "Revenez un peu plus tard, mademoiselle. A dix-neuf heures et demie! Nous serons prêts pour vous accueillir!" Come back a little later, mademoiselle! At 7:30! We will be ready to welcome you....

I thought of the cinder-block room at the club where we all choked down our dinners, some of us clocking in early to serve people who wanted to dine before the formal room officially opened. I compared our bare Formica table in that sullen room to the linen-draped table amid the flowers and vines on the terrace. The carafes of wine. The pots of food shared family style—certainly, this wasn't tournedos Rossini they were eating, but it was no dinosaur bones or crusty leftover chicken salad. The cheese. The salad. And the little cups of espresso and the little sugar cubes and the little spoons, all served on a tray by the proprietress, likely her firm but polite way of saying, "Dinner is over." Yes, it was time to get to work, but how nice to be reminded via a cup of espresso rather than the loud thud of a time clock clicking off the minutes in a windowless break room.

That night we did, of course, dine at that restaurant. We sat on the terrace and had a kind of hearty beef daube, followed by a green salad that was dressed with a vinaigrette so garlicky that it almost stung, in a bright, zingy, refreshing way that was perfect after the meaty stew. We splurged on fromage *et* dessert (rather than fromage *ou* dessert). I don't exactly remember the cheeses, but they were good, I'm sure. What I do remember is that at one point during the cheese course, our wineglasses and our carafes were empty. Seeing our empty glasses, a jovial old waiter snagged for us the quarter-full carafe of wine left on a nearby table recently vacated by another couple. "Faut du vin avec le fromage," he said. Indeed, you can't have cheese without wine.

It occurred to me that the staff seemed to operate from a kind of pact: they had had their turn sitting down at the table and being nourished and cared for. When it was our turn to sit at the table, the promise was that we would be in equally good hands.

Our second day in Avignon, getting back on budget, we found ourselves on the banks of the river, eating a ham-and-cheese baguette sandwich and drinking tepid mineral water from a plastic bottle underneath a feathery tree in the warm spring sun, overlooking the wide green-gray water below.

The night before had me thinking that day of how genuine and dignified most servers were in the restaurants we had dined in throughout Europe. They seemed to move through their work with an authoritativeness and pride that I longed for but didn't always feel when waiting tables.

Six weeks into our backpacking trip, as I sat on the banks of the Rhône that day, I was happier than I'd ever been in my life. What luck, just to be somewhere beautiful and looking forward to another walk around an old city, another café to kill time in before we had another budget meal to savor, followed by a night of love and affection in our eleven-dollars-a-night hotel, spotlessly clean but with threadbare carpet, dated floral wallpaper, and warped in-swing casing windows open to the sweet night air. It overjoyed me, what twenty dollars a day could give us. It made me so sad to think that the daily pleasures that any waiter in France could enjoy were so far absent from my own waitressing life in Des Moines.

Later, a mild curiosity led me to ask a group of young women sitting nearby, "Quel est le nom de ce fleuve?" What is the name of that river?

They smiled at my foreign pronunciation but were eager to answer. "C'est le Rhône," they told me.

I thought of how, coming in on the train, we had seen vineyards with their first yellow-green spring leaves along the slopes of this river. And it suddenly came to me—*This is the Rhône, and I am sitting on its slopes, and that means I am here on les côtes du Rhône.* I thought of all the bottles of Côtes du Rhône wine we had served at the club, and how far I had been from the joy of knowing that there's a specific place in the world where this wine is made, and it's made only in this one place in the world and nowhere else.

Why had no one ever told me such a wondrous, matterful thing?

That night, we went out for a four-course, 55-franc prix-fixe menu (pâté, steak au poivre verte, fromage, glace). But rather than getting our usual pichet de vin, we ordered the least expensive bottle of Côtes du Rhône on the list. It tasted like the joy of knowing something good has settled into your soul and will be there forever.

I realized during the trip that my lifetime goal would be to re-arrange a modest but sweet life around more moments like those I had on the côtes du Rhône. I also knew that if I stayed at the club one minute longer than was absolutely necessary to make enough money to escape, I might just forget there were moments like these to live for. I might start blowing smoke in the faces of my coworkers.

We got home at the end of May. Each of us spent six hundred dollars less than we had budgeted for the trip, but that wasn't enough to get us very far. Dave went back to counting art supplies at his brother's store. I reluctantly went back to the club for night shifts but worked days at a university bookstore. I was working about sixty-five hours a week, hoping that I'd soon be able to get, as they say, anywhere but here.

One day in midsummer, on a rare afternoon that we both had off, we searched for a place where we could have a drink outside. We were missing the pleasures of the sidewalk cafés of Europe, but we could only think of one place that had outside dining: TGI Fridays, out in a western suburb just off the freeway.

We asked to be seated outside, where it soon grew stifling hot. The large and inelegant black iron tables were meant to seat six to eight; the table umbrellas were ill-positioned from the sun that beat down on the pavement, making me wistfully recall how the expert waiters at sidewalk cafés in Europe constantly monitored the ever-moving angles of the light, maneuvering tables and umbrellas throughout the day to make sure customers always had a shady spot to sit. We grew hot and cranky before a server even had the chance to take our order. We looked at the menu and realized that a good drink would cost at least one hour's pay after tax and tip, and that one would not be enough. We took in the view of the cars zipping along the freeway, our ears picked up its incessant whoosh, and we realized how little we'd enjoy the overpriced drinks.

"Let's get out of here," said Dave.

"Where should we go?" I asked. I started to name a few bars.

"No," he said. "I mean, it's time to leave Des Moines. This is no way to live."

It took us a few more months, but on November 1 of that year, we packed up a little U-Haul Mini Mover and moved to Brooklyn in search of a different life, even if we had no idea what that would be. A friend of a friend had helped us land an apartment in a commercially (but not residentially) zoned brownstone on a beat stretch of Schermerhorn Street. We arrived without jobs, but within two weeks, I was working as a bilingual secretary for a French bank in Rockefeller Plaza, and Dave was working an entry-level job for Ziff Davis publishing. We both got our jobs by answering ads in the *New York Times*.

Although the year and a half I spent at the club were not the happiest of my days, I'm grateful for the experience. When I became a restaurant reviewer, I was well-versed in the ins and outs of fine dining. I knew what should happen in the dining rooms of high-end restaurants. Certainly, I didn't expect the kind of exacting French service we effected at a private club, yet when paying top dollar at a splurgy restaurant, I did look for some of its hallmarks—thoughtful timings, the clearing of plates, the keeping track of silverware—along with an overall sense of precision and care.

I had also gained a deep understanding of how diminishing the work can feel to those in the industry. I understood why, for instance, a waiter might linger at our table chatting with us longer than we might have wished: he simply wanted to be seen. I've been there. The club helped me approach the job of reviewing restaurants with a mix of high standards and genuine compassion.

SALAD DAYS IN NEW YORK CITY

While the New York stretch of my life, with its foolhardy romances, artistic awakenings, and a truly awful job at a women's magazine, deserves a book of its own, the culinary strides I made while living there are worth mentioning here.

I had moved there to work in publishing (which I eventually did), but because I landed in the city with very little money, I took the first job I could find. I worked for the International Banking Group of Société Générale, a French bank then located at 50 Rockefeller Plaza. My official title was bilingual secretary, even though I spoke French like an American cow on a Spanish prairie, as the French sometimes say about non-native speakers. Not that anyone I worked for would ever say such a thing to me.

While I was the lowest in the hierarchy—typing, filing, and answering the phone sometimes in French and sometimes in English—I was treated with a reserved cheerfulness by the impeccably dressed bank executives I worked for. No one ever made fun of my French, even if they would gently correct me now and then.

One of the great perks of working for Société Générale was that every so often, we would be treated to a luncheon in the executive dining room. Understatedly furnished in heavy dark wood, with windows overlooking Rockefeller Plaza, this mini restaurant had its own French chef and a dedicated waiter who wasn't French but was equally exacting. The elegant room was designed as a place for the executives to discreetly entertain potential banking clients with the best possible food, wine, and service. While I would often make reservations for the executives at other revered high-end French restaurants in our area—most often Lutèce and Prunelle—the private dining room was what the tops would reserve for meetings with clients who needed some extra finessing or who wanted to keep potential banking relationships private.

I loved spotting the menus, written in French, and if I didn't know a term, I'd ask. It was in this way that, in addition to dull French words for banking (which I've long since forgotten), I learned culinary terms ranging from "vacherin" and "ris de veau" to "sanglier" and "salmis," and of course, words to describe all kinds of tournedos (Beaugency, Clamart, Rossini, and more).

All this learning would have been wistful window-shopping had I not had the great luck to dine in the splendid dining room myself. Every few months, someone would host a holiday party, a welcome fête for a new employee in our group, or a send-off for an expatriate heading back to France, and even the secretaries would get to dine upstairs.

I had never tasted such delicacies as lobster à l'Américaine, the rich meat in its slick oil and Cognac-laced sauce sparked by the lilt of tomatoes and white wine; I'd never dreamed a fish could taste like the most opulent of scallops, as did the skate, served with citrusy brown-butter caper sauce. I had, until that point, never even tasted capers. And since when did ice cream taste so good? With its poached pear, deep chocolate sauce, whipped cream that had an almost buttery edge, plus a few sugared violets—the poire belle Hélène remains to this day one of my all-time favorite desserts.

I never pretended for a moment that I was so sophisticated as to know what any of these things were. Rather, I let my joy and astonishment show at every turn. Once, when we were served cèpes à la Bordelaise (fresh porcini mushrooms sautéed simply with shallots, parsley, and lemon juice), I did not hide how over the moon I was at discovering such rich, earthy flavors robed in their vibrant sauce.

"But mademoiselle," said Solange, an elegant middle-aged French executive secretary, "Surely you've had cèpes before?"

"I haven't!" I said. "So why is it that none of you ever told me about these things?"

There are people in the world who might use their superior knowledge of food to, let's face it, lord some kind of status over someone else. We've all met those people. But my French colleagues around the table those days did no such thing. Instead, they radiated a kind of joy, likely from having enjoyed a long stretch of good wine and good food, along with gratitude for growing up knowing about such things, all mixed with the pleasure of sharing something wonderful with someone who not only truly appreciated it but was also very happy to let you know they did.

Back down on the street level, I was learning much about food and cooking. Though what came to my table in our humble old apartment in Brooklyn was by no means tournedos Calmart and lobster à l'Américaine, the food improved by the week.

The mid- to late 1980s were the stir-fry years; back in Des Moines, I had bought a remaindered Chinese cookbook for a few bucks but could never find the ingredients I needed to cook the recipes. Suddenly, hoisin and oyster sauce, five-spice powder, rice wine, and sesame oil were available at the Korean-run greengrocer a block from our apartment. Using the wok my roommates had gifted me in college, I made all the popular standbys of the time, from cashew chicken and Mongolian beef to fried rice. Nearly everyone I knew could turn out these popularized dishes, which likely weren't the most true-to-China versions, but they tasted fresh and exotic to me after a long day of typing and filing at the office followed by the grubby commute home on the subway.

But who knew I could cook French? Pierre Franey made it so.

I never missed the Wednesday food pages of the *New York Times*, as that's when Pierre Franey's 60-Minute Gourmet column would run. Each week, Franey would offer one main course and one side dish that, together, could be put on the table in sixty minutes or less. The recipes were generally French in nature—after all, French-born Franey was a classically trained chef who had overseen the kitchen at the restaurant Le Pavillon. Yet his recipes revealed an everyday, easy side of French cooking that I never imagined I could pull off so simply and beautifully at home.

I loved reading his column on the subway ride home and then figuring out my shopping list; on the way from the Borough Hall subway stop to my apartment, I would stop at the butcher or fish market, the greengrocer, and the wine shop. Once home, I'd have dinner on the table quickly for Dave and our roommate, Neal (aka Poem-Belly, an old friend we lived with to help pay the rent).

It was sheer pleasure to go into these little shops where, unlike at the battened-down supermarkets I had shopped at in Iowa, you could actually smell the wares—the gamy meats at the butcher, the fishy and sea-air scent of the fishmonger, the citrusy aromas of the greengrocer. The butcher shop, tucked to one side of a porn theater called the Cin-Art (ha), especially stole my heart, with two exceedingly jovial older men behind the counter who never, ever seemed annoyed that I'd just buy a half pound of ground veal here or one single chicken breast there. They'd slow down to answer my questions about meats that were specified in the recipes I was trying to cook, helping me figure out a cut I could use if they didn't have the one I requested, even if they had to trim off such a tiny piece for me that it was hardly worth their time.

Nearly thirty years later, I went back to the block where the butcher shop had been; of course, I knew it would no longer be there, and that the men who ran it were probably long retired or even long gone. I expected to be sad, but I didn't expect to feel the outright grief that washed over me when I saw the whole block had been demolished and rebuilt and was now the site of a sleek mega Barnes & Noble bookstore. It kind of made me even miss the Cin-Art.

I also dined out as much as I could on a salary that started at $13,500 a year and never rose above $21,000. I tasted my first round of clams casino at Lenny's Clam Bar, my first chicken Francese at Queen Restaurant, and this marvelous thing called smoked fresh mozzarella at a deli in Red Hook. From a boilerplate platter of chips and salsa at an average Mexican restaurant on the corner of Atlantic and Court, I got my inaugural, head-turning taste of an herb that tasted vaguely soapy, lightly minty, a little bit spicy, and wholly fresh.

"What *is* this stuff?" I asked Poem-Belly.

He looked at the leafy light-green herb in a blob of otherwise unremarkable salsa and said, "Oh that? That's cilantro."

Unlike Solange in the dining room of Société Générale, he did not express any surprise that I had never tasted such a thing; he was a native New Yorker who had been dragged kicking and screaming to Iowa for high school when his mom and dad split up and his mom had moved to Des Moines to work at the major publisher there. He had hightailed it back east the moment he could, then cycled in and out of school and odd jobs. By the time we were living with him, he was in his mid-twenties but just a sophomore in college.

Neal had the insatiable hunger for good food and many other sensual things that most poets have (it's why we called him Poem-Belly), and as such he knew where to find great foods that didn't cost much. In Brooklyn, he turned us on to true Hungarian goulash, Jewish rugelach, lemon curd on English scones, the best grape leaves on Atlantic Avenue, smoked salmon omelets, fried egg and cheese sandwiches on toasted onion rolls, spanakopita—even a killer-good meatloaf at a dingy old-man bar-minicafeteria on Court Street. And on Sundays, we'd all head out to brunch at a place called Capulet's on Montague Street, where I finally found the sidewalk experience I had so yearned for and could not find in Des Moines.

A year and a half into my stint at the French bank, I began to wonder what I was doing working at a French bank. For the first year, I was thrilled to be employed anywhere that let me live, however frugally, in New York City and didn't require me to wear a uniform or punch a time clock. For the first year, that was good enough.

Still, I always read the help wanted ads in the *New York Times*, and one day, I saw a job for an editorial assistant at an upmarket women's magazine. I answered the ad, and soon I was working as the assistant to a senior editor who insisted on calling me "Winifred" rather than "Wini" because "It's just *too* midwestern to shorten names." When I politely insisted that really, I preferred "Wini," she started trying out other nicknames, and somehow "Munchkin" stuck.

Strangely, she didn't seem to have a lot to do during the day; rather, she spent a lot of time sitting and smoking cigarettes and flipping through magazines and trade papers, now and then pointing out the people she ostensibly knew personally.

My days were spent mostly sitting outside Carolyn's office looking through magazines and scouting out stories of people who might be good subjects for our own pages. When I wasn't doing that, I fetched her coffee, lunch, and personal items such as cigarettes. I remember spending one afternoon doing almost nothing, and then at 5 p.m., when it was time for me to go home, she asked me to buy her cigarettes from the newsstand.

When I told her the newsstand in the building would now be closed, she told me to walk five blocks to the stand at Grand Central Station. I was lucky if I made it back to Brooklyn by 7 p.m., even though I had done pretty much nothing all day.

The only thing that made the days worthwhile were the nights: the stir-fries; the simple, splendid food that Pierre Franey had taught me to cook; the forays into cheap Brooklyn dining with Dave and Poem-Belly.

One day, Carolyn invited her staff of assistant and associate editors and me, the editorial assistant, to lunch at the Algonquin; she asked me to reserve a large round table in the Rose Room because, she said, it would be our own "round table"—a latter-day iteration of the circle of famed writers and wits of the 1920s who gathered there daily.

The food was forgettable, and the conversation was worse. They talked of one senior editor's body odor. "I think we should enlist someone to snag a bottle of Magie Noire from the beauty department and leave it on her desk as a hint," said one at the table. They gossiped about another editor who dressed too young for her age and swore like a sailor, even though, as someone else said, everyone knew "women over thirty should not swear." Someone claimed she was certain one of the editors (whether food, accessories, beauty, or fashion, I don't remember) was, in fact, "illiterate" and "couldn't spell her own name." And, added someone, did you see what the new editor had worn that day? A tight-fitting brown (*brown!*) polyester dress that made her look "like a cow."

Yes, I know that the famous Algonquin Round Table was also called "the Vicious Circle," that mordant wit was the order of the day. But there was no wit, just a kind of middle school meanness. Feeling like the corny midwesterner at a table of sophisticates, I began to wonder if there was some secret code I just was not getting. Was I being a self-righteous scold for not finding the conversation very funny? Maybe I needed to grow up, or, more accurately, regress to middle school.

During those years in New York, the table had become, for me, a kind of sanctuary, a place where the pummeling of the most hostile parts of the city could be held at bay, if only for a while. When making the reservation, I had envisioned the kind of lovely meal and jovial conversations I had experienced with my colleagues at Société Générale. Was my growing frustration over missing out on something potentially meaningful just too naïve for words?

Finally, an assistant editor, Ivy League educated but originally from the South, spoke up in a soothing but firm southern accent and said she'd had enough. "We sound like some kind of snooty clique at an exclusive summer camp," she said. The party grew sullen, but I breathed more easily. While I was grateful she put an end to the maliciousness, I was also sad I had not had the temerity to do so myself.

If you're in a job where you find yourself unable to speak up when others are being stupidly vicious, then that job is probably a bad fit. Especially if you pretty much hate the job anyway.

I lasted exactly six months at the magazine. When I left, I was twenty-five; most of my friends (aside from Poem-Belly) had moved on from entry-level clerical jobs and were working as associate editors or associate publicists or copywriters. But I knew that without any significant editing or writing experience I could point to, I'd likely have to start all over. Once again, the *New York Times* came through; I answered a job ad for a marketing assistant at Oxford University Press, where I'd work for almost the rest of my twenties, quickly advancing to copywriter. A few years later, I handled the marketing and publicity for the press's journals.

While it was by no means exciting or glamorous to write and edit catalogs and brochures on scholarly journals covering topics from Asian art to molluscan studies, the job was interesting in a nerdy way and also gave me the editorial experience I needed. I was surrounded by smart, funny people who'd made their way to the press from places as far as Santa Barbara and as close as the Bronx. It was a quiet pocket of mellowness between Fifth and Madison Avenues in Midtown, and frankly, I loved it.

By then, Dave and I had married and moved to an overpriced one-bedroom on the Upper East Side. Poem-Belly had found his first of three wives and had moved deeper into Brooklyn, to Red Hook. Our New York years sped by while we worked long days and filled the nights with all the things childless young people do in New York—plays, ballets, rock concerts, and boutique music shows, and of course, the eating of everything, from Cuban black beans and rice to Ukrainian pierogies, from new-on-the-scene sushi and trendy-at-the-time Cajun to coquilles St.-Jacques in the aging French restaurants near the Theater District. I finally seized some differences between northern and southern Italian cuisine, between Provençal and Parisian.

But one day we hit a wall. As we moved up in our careers, we were working harder and longer, yet (being in publishing) barely making enough money to scrape by. Night after night, I'd either cook (with energy that waned by the day), or we'd use our telescope, which we had originally bought to gaze at the stars on our rooftop in Brooklyn, to check out the specials listed in the window of the pub across the street. We'd eat and drink, then fall, exhausted, into bed. Métro, boulot, dodo, as the French say: subway, job, sleep. And we were only twenty-eight.

Sometimes, especially if the Mets were playing, we'd go to a bar on First Avenue called the Tumble Inn. We'd sit and drink beer and sometimes I'd play Pac-Man to unwind. One night Dave said, "You know, we can sit and drink beer at a dive bar and watch baseball and play Pac-Man anywhere in the country, without spending half our paychecks on rent." We soon made plans to part ways with the city.

I was able to rustle up a stint at Oxford University Press in Oxford, England, and we soon offloaded most of our possessions and shipped a few boxes to the UK.

For the very last meal we were to eat as true New Yorkers, bona fide residents of the city, we went to a brand-new Italian deli in the neighborhood and ordered a couple sandwiches to take back to the empty apartment before handing the keys to the landlord and pulling out of town forever.

As we were picking up and paying for the sandwiches, the man behind the counter handed me a lengthy to-go menu and said, "Please come back!"

"Thanks," I said, passing the menu back to him, "but we're moving out of the city today, leaving for good. I'm afraid this will be our first and last time eating here." I didn't want him to waste a handsomely printed four-color menu on someone who wouldn't use it; I didn't want him to wonder why we never came back.

"Oh!" he said, turning around and grabbing a little tin of Italian pastille candies from behind the counter. He quickly unpeeled a sticker with the deli's name on it, stuck it to the bottom of the tin, and handed it to me.

"A gift! For you to remember us by!" he said. "Good luck!"

I still have that tin, a gesture of goodwill from a restaurateur who had nothing more to gain from us. It was this little gift that tipped my ongoing love–hate relationship with New York firmly and forever in the love camp.

MY FRANCE PROBLEM

In 1988, we moved to Oxford, England, where I worked at the headquarters of Oxford University Press. The following year, Dave and I headed to Ann Arbor, Michigan, where Dave completed graduate school. In 1991, we moved back to our hometown of Des Moines, where Dave began his career as an English professor, and I eventually fell into food writing.

In 1992 and 1993, Dave and I traveled to the South of France for most of the month of June. We didn't know it then, but for the next twenty-five years, summer trips to France would become an almost yearly tradition for us.

For our trip in the summer of 1995, we decided to take France to the next level. Instead of staying in hotels, we'd look for an apartment with a kitchen, something few Americans did in the days before VRBO. With no way of knowing what we'd find, we budgeted enough for thirty-dollar-a-night hotels in case that plan didn't work.

We touched down in Nice and took a train to Beaulieu-sur-Mer, a town on the French Riviera between Nice and Monaco. At the time, it was a somewhat down-at-the-heels town with a defunct casino, but the setting was spectacular: the Belle Epoque buildings sometimes showed their wear with peeling paint, but they were framed by a crescent of azure waters to the south and the sheer pinkish-green cliffs of the Alpes-Maritimes to the north. We knew we'd have better luck finding something affordable in this less traveled town than if we went for the big names like Cannes and St. Tropez.

We walked from the train station to an estate agent just across the street, and less than an hour later, we were unpacking our cases in an apartment we had rented for the month.

The Studio Benvenuto was in an old Belle Epoque building above our estate agent's offices. His family owned the three-story building, and his ninety-something mother lived on the floor below us. This modest studio apartment had one large living room with two daybeds that could be pushed together for a double bed at night; the in-swing floor-to-ceiling windows opened to the balustrade of a Juliet balcony, adding airiness and Mediterranean light to the room. The sheer cliffs were visible from the balcony, and while it also faced the train station, there was charm and energy in that—the small old station was housed in a white-washed, tile-roofed building, and the comings and goings of people brought views of the daily life that we always loved. The separate kitchen had a tiny old gas stove and a small fridge (typical of France, because you went to the market for fresh food every day) but plenty of counter space. Best of all, from the kitchen, you could look out the window and see the sea about five blocks away.

This charming little studio cost us thirty dollars a night, which was about half the price of a beat cabin we had rented the summer before in northern Minnesota. With me as a freelancer and Dave as an academic with summers off, we had, at last, arranged our lives around the possibility of as much travel time as possible. And with our discovery of the Studio Benvenuto, we had found an affordable way of doing so. Even after taking airfare into consideration, France was clearly the choice for our budget and for the amount of time we wanted to travel.

And there was, of course, the fact that we loved it. There's the sea, with its waters so impossibly blue that only a few painters have ever been able to capture its color; in lesser hands, that blue always looks mawkish rather than magical. The water is always cool and clear, and I've never felt anything but sheer giddiness jumping into it on a hot day. In fact, every time I jump into the Mediterranean, it feels all new, like it's the very first time. I once saw an elderly woman being half-carried, half-guided into the sea by two younger women; she had that lost, worried expression of someone suffering from dementia, but once in the water, she let out a gasp of recognition and delight, and suddenly she seemed to possess all the joy of once again being twenty years old on the Cote d'Azur.

Those sheer cliffs at Beaulieu-sur-Mer show colors of pale marblelike pink and scrubby green during the day; at night, the mountains all but disappear, save for the way the streetlamps sparkle on the Moyenne Corniche (the middle road), looking like a necklace of diamonds hanging in the dark sky. If you dare, take perilous roads—marked in white on the highly detailed regional Michelin maps—to the less trampled perched villages, such as Peille and Peillon; have lunch at one of the few restaurants there; then walk around the rocky village in the stone-silent afternoon, catching glimpses of the rugged terrain and the lush mountain passes beyond.

Yes, there are plenty of sights to see—a Rothschild mansion here, a medieval chateau there, Roman ruins, Monaco, and even the gates of the Villa Nellcôte, where the Rolling Stones famously stayed while working on their masterpiece, *Exile on Main Street*. Yet we usually did only two or three sites every month; the rest of the time was spent immersed in the daily life we once loved watching and of which we were now partaking.

For the first few trips, I brought my tattered copy of Pierre Franey's *60-Minute Gourmet* and had a fine old time heading to the morning markets, sniffing melons at the produce stands, going back and forth with the butcher about his best alternatives to the American cuts of meat called for in my book. I'd choose cheeses at the cheesemonger, pick up the daily bread at the boulangerie, and find some lovely little desserts at the patisserie, somewhere along the line picking up the *Herald Tribune* at the tabac, settling into a café to casually pour over the pages. It was amazing how long it took to get through the thin editions when across the street in the square there was so much else to see—young boys kicking a soccer ball, grandmothers holding the hands of toddlers taking uneasy steps atop short stone walls, passersby, the sunlight shifting as it fell through the leaves of the plane trees.

In later years, my cooking would be much more contemporary, sometimes springing from the pages of current French cooking magazines, where I'd discover the way busy French cooks (who aren't spending their days café-dwelling and beach-hopping) put fresh, vivid meals on the table. Yet very often, I needed no recipes at all. When great ingredients and artisanal products are always within steps of your door, it's easy to dine well at home.

Yet we loved dining out, too. Beaulieu-sur-Mer is just a few stone's throws from Italy, so in addition to the wonderful coastal, Provençal, and traditional French cooking—from pâtés and pureed fish soup with crazy-garlicky aioli to olive-studded beef stews and simply grilled sea bream—we'd find plenty of thin-crust pizza and pasta, such as a divine lasagna with a slather of creamy béchamel sauce between the layers. For dessert, an apricot tart or crème caramel might share the billing with tiramisu and semifreddo.

We became regulars at quite a few restaurants in town, so much so that a proprietor, seeing us pass by his place one morning, chased us down the sidewalk and told us to be sure to come to dinner that weekend: they were serving Sisteron lamb, a superior pasture-raised meat from elsewhere in Provence. We indeed partook, reveling in tender, rosy meat, with its gentle but persistent lamby flavor, grilled with olive oil, rosemary, and thyme.

One year, we spent our final night of that trip dining at our favorite little restaurant, La Pignatelle, where we had become habitués. We happened to tell our server that we were flying home the next day. After we paid our bill, as we got up to leave the restaurant, the proprietress asked us to stay a minute in the dining room. A few moments later, she led us into the foyer, where the staff—our waiter, the cooks in their white toques, smart-looking young waitresses in their tight black miniskirts and white blouses, the proprietress in her flowy dress—were all lined up to shake our hands and bid us farewell, until next year. At the end of the line, the proprietresses presented us with a bottle of wine so that we could have a taste of France once home.

This, at a place where we rarely spent more than thirty dollars per person for a three- or four-course meal including a bottle of wine between us. Where we never even left a gratuity (service was always included in the price). Even today, the new incarnation of this restaurant continues to serve three-course menus starting at thirty euros per person, tax and service included—though these days, some diners are inclined to leave a few euros for a gratuity.

This was and still is my France. Often, when people tell me about their travels in France, they're quick to talk about their Michelin-starred dining experiences. I've been to such temples of fine dining, and while I'm always dazzled by the food in the moment, they're never what I remember in any deep and meaningful way back home.

Frankly, I'll save my splurges for the U.S.—I honestly believe that high-end dining in America can be every bit as extraordinary as high-end dining in France. In the realm of gastronomy (food as art), I doubt I ever had anything in France better than the meals I had, for example, at Charlie Trotter, Tru, and Spiaggia in Chicago. Rather, I go to France for what I can't find at home. I'm rarely more tickled than when I'm tucking into one of those thoughtful three-course meals that are affordable for schoolteachers, secretaries, bus drivers, plumbers, and postal workers alike: perhaps a homemade soup, pâté, or colorful mix of raw, beautifully dressed vegetable salads to start; steak frites, confit de canard, pork chops in mustard sauce, or trout meunière for the main course; followed by a choice of the fruit tart of the day, crème caramel, or a couple scoops of lovely ice cream or sorbet (a scoop each of cassis and vanilla never fails to thrill me). Such menus rarely cost more than fifteen euros at lunch or twenty euros at dinner.

Of course, sometimes we do splurge, but never in that four-hundred dollars per person, three-Michelin star way. French restaurants manage to pull off a splendid experience for a price that, while not an every day or even an every month thing for most people, can certainly be an affordable luxury when you're feeling flush. These days, once you hit the sixty-five-euro mark per person, you'll likely be in for fascinating creations that sometimes require three lines of text to describe—for example, sea bass with a sauce flavored with ginger vinegar and bear's garlic (i.e., wild garlic), served with fava beans and celery root with Sarawak white pepper. And believe you me, I love every bite of these occasional extravaganzas.

But the truth is, you simply do not have to spend a lot to dine well in France. Yet when you do go for that occasional sixty-five euros per person meal, it's a pretty sure bet that the strikingly imaginative food, crafted with precise, high-spirited details, will be served with an exactitude and expertise that dignifies the work of the kitchen. One of my favorite, most telling moments of high-end service in France happened at one such restaurant in the Vézère Valley in southwestern France. At one point in the meal, I absentmindedly picked up a piece of unused cutlery on the table and for no reason at all put it down in another spot within my table setting. A few moments later, when the server came by to pour us some wine, he stopped, put the bottle back on the trivet, and stared at my place settings for a few seconds with a look of great consternation. Something was not right, he knew it, and for him, it was like solving a puzzle. Suddenly, he cracked the code: he picked up the wayward fork and gently but assuredly put it back in its proper place. All being right with the world again, he went back to his task and genially poured our wine.

Some might call this kind of service uptight, and occasionally, it can feel that way. But usually, such rigor is about care, not pretentiousness. It's about making sure all is as it should be, at least for the time you're sitting at the table.

A few years ago, I became acquainted with a French chef who was working in Iowa. I casually asked him if he thought he could find a job for me waiting tables at a fine restaurant in France (it was, for a while, a dream of mine). He said he was pretty sure he could. I felt proud for a moment, saying, "Wow—do you really think my French is up to the job?" He looked at me like I was an idiot and said, "You don't understand. If you went to France to train to be a server at a fine-dining establishment, you would not even be allowed to talk to a customer for at least a year."

Yikes. That made my one-week training at the private dining club look way less than adequate. And it shows how seriously the French take restaurant service at that level.

Of course, I didn't always experience (or even expect) such rigor when dining out, as I generally didn't go to the sixty-five euros per person places. At the humbler venues where I dined, service would be caring and careful, though certainly not so rigorous that the server would be disconcerted by a misplaced fork.

Yet every once in a while, I would encounter a kind of precision, even in the humbler places, that would astound me. At an everyday brasserie next door to our budget but long-gone Hôtel de Nevers in Paris, a friend and I sat at the zinc counter having a late-morning café express. We saw the barman prepping mustard pots for the day's lunch service of steak frites, poulet frites, omelets, croque monsieurs, and other casual café offerings. We watched as he carefully spooned the Dijon mustard into each little brown pot, assiduously wiping clean any spills. Then he meticulously placed each little plastic spatula in the mustard, near the rim of each pot, with each spatula positioned at exactly the same depth. My friend and I had been chatting away, but suddenly, we both fell silent, mesmerized by his movements as if we were watching a graceful athlete, a virtuoso musician, or anyone at the top of their game. I couldn't help but think of my own days filling grungy ketchup bottles in the back room of Country Kitchen and compare the delight and dignity he took in doing his task to my lack of the same as I did mine. The cultures in which we did our work were worlds apart.

Dave and I were also often struck by just how much joy restaurateurs and their staff took in ensuring the diner's pleasure. At an unassuming inn in a tiny town in the eastern Pyrenees, the proprietor asked us to let him know in advance if we'd be taking dinner in their little dining room. We decided to reserve our first meal to see how it went. After the simple but everything-we-wanted meal—starting with garbure (a rustic ham-vegetable-bean soup of the region), moving on to roast chicken with piperade, and finishing with delicate slices of young sheep's milk cheese and sweet cherry jam—we told the proprietor we would indeed like to take our remaining dinners in his dining room. I can still see him smiling at the news with immense pride and unmistakable joy.

Another night, somewhere in the Gers in southwestern France, we did not, as is our usual habit, order a fixed price, multicourse menu. We had been traveling around the southwest a few weeks, and we were gavé. The term literally means "force-fed" and refers to the way regional ducks are force-fed to make foie gras, yet locals also use it to mean when they themselves have eaten to excess. It was the perfect term for us, having enjoyed a few too many foie gras this and confit de canard that, cassoulets, bone-marrow sauces, and other hearty regional dishes.

So we enjoyed an appetizer and a main course but declined dessert. The server didn't seem too put out by this, but a few moments later, the proprietor came up to our table and asked us if everything had been all right. We told him we had enjoyed our meal very much.

"But you didn't order dessert," he said sadly. It seemed that not ordering dessert was a comment on everything that came before—as if we didn't have enough confidence in the kitchen to feel that the final course would be worthwhile.

We explained that we were from the United States, we'd been traveling around the southwest for a few weeks, and we just weren't used to eating three-course meals night after night, no matter how wonderful they were.

He seemed satisfied with our response and asked if we would care, instead, for an Armagnac offert (on the house). We told him yes, and when he asked which kind, we told him we didn't know Armagnac well enough to choose. He stepped away, then back he came with several bottles representing the three distinct regions where the spirit is made. He stood there and gave us our own little Armagnac tasting. Later, he proceeded to get out a map of the region and show us where some off-the-beaten path Gallo-Roman ruins could be found. Clearly, he did not want us to leave the Gers without experiencing as much as he could offer up for us to taste and do.

What, then, is my France problem? To put it bluntly, it was having to come back to Des Moines and write fairly and honestly about Des Moines restaurants, and to avoid feeling like an annoying, overprivileged bourgeois snob when faced with another first course consisting of a bucket of lettuce, a main dish sided with a pile of pasta or a heap of garlic mashed potatoes, and a dessert of a big chocolate-goo thing or thuddingly heavy cheesecake.

I always tried to ease back into the Des Moines dining scene by seeking out what we did best. Wide awake from jet lag, we'd go over to the Drake Diner the moment it opened for bacon and eggs and hash browns and pancakes that tasted like home and that were a welcome shift from six weeks of the rarely changing breakfast menu of café au lait, croissants, and tartine (baguette, jam, butter).

I'd go somewhere for a medium-rare cut of prime rib, or maybe a thick ribeye, and revel in its opulent marbling and big beefy flavor. I'd head to Thai Flavors for a nutty-sweet-sour-spicy tom kha kai; I'd go to one of our unassuming Mexican restaurants for simple street-style chorizo tacos, unmistakably fresh not only thanks to the fresh ingredients but for having gone from the grill to your hands in seconds. Oh, and yes, I'd go to the "other" kind of Mexican places—those that serve big, cheesy combo plates and stellar margaritas, because . . . big, cheesy combo plates and stellar margaritas. I'd go out for barbecue at the famous (thanks to Guy Fieri) Flying Mango or one of our other admirable spots, and at a midcentury Italian American place called Noah's Ark, I'd feel a certain comfort in the style of pizza I was raised on (not thin crust, not thick crust, but with crispness and chew all its own).

I'd go to a more modern Italian American place, Sam & Gabe's, and have the city's renowned specialty: steak de burgo, a tender herb-crusted filet served in a pool of garlic-butter sauce. Or, I'd have their cannelloni, the most luscious on the planet, stuffed with veal, pork, and beef and slathered with béchamel on one side, red sauce on the other, for a wonderful combination of richness and zip. At a downtown hotspot called Centro, I'd tuck into chicken Francese, a buttery, lemon-sparked dish with a name that means "French" in Italian, but that I'd never seen in France or Italy—because it's the kind of 100 percent Italian American classic about which chef-partner

George Formaro is fiercely and justifiably proud. A big juicy burger at Star Bar, my favorite local bar-grill, could also make me pretty happy, especially when I'd see some of my favorite people in town piling in and out of the neighborhood joint.

Yes, there were a few months' worth of restaurants to revel in once home. Trouble was, I'd already written about most of them. There was that bugaboo of the two-year window that precluded me from writing about Centro or Sam & Gabe's for no other reason than I wanted to eat at these places. While I would certainly time it so that I'd have a shoo-in or two to write about when I got back, sooner or later I'd be faced with the inevitable bucket of lettuce followed by the usual plates of undistinguished overabundance. After prying my mind open with a crowbar, I'd remember that this was Iowa, and that these types of restaurateurs were simply giving their clientele what they wanted—what else could account for the popularity of such venues? I'd simply try my best to tell people what to expect, even if I thought they deserved better.

What was truly tough going were the more ambitious restaurants, especially those that strove to serve the kind of French, Italian, or Mediterranean food I'd enjoyed at its source just a few weeks earlier. I would love more than anything to be able to say that such places compared favorably to what I'd found abroad. But the truth was much more complicated.

Certainly, our most talented chefs made beautiful plates from food they'd thoughtfully sourced. Very often, it was the best fine dining our city had to offer, and nothing made me happier than to say so in print. At French-focused Bistro Montage, chef-restaurateur Enosh Kelley artfully crafted his own distinct modern-bistro cuisine, deftly steering the territory between cozily French and refreshingly fascinating: an appetizer of cherry-duck sausage, delicately sliced and fanned alongside a sweet-tart onion confit; a main course of a plump rack of lamb and demi-glace, with spring vegetables and a black-truffle potato croquette; and desserts that sent me over the moon, particularly the dacquoise, buttercream-filled meringue layers graced with chocolate ganache and ground almonds. It was that splendid rarity among local desserts—one that made you feel happy to have eaten it, rather than done-in and depressed.

Of course, I also admired chefs who brought equal expertise and precision to their food but veered well off the classic French path. At Alba, Jason Simon was a master at combining worldly inspiration with down-home touches and local ingredients for his refined cooking: a New York strip arrived with a bright chimichurri and sweet-corn succotash, while a moist, gleaming-white halibut was detailed with aromatic saffron, fresh-picked zucchini, and decadent crescents of crisp-fried duck skin.

Other spots could do similarly great meals, and again and again, I'd think, *It's pretty amazing how far this city's culinary scene has come.*

And yet . . . inconsistency proved the undoing of many a meal. A place you'd revel in one week (in print, even!) would let you down hard a few months later. I ventured into one of my very favorite New American venues one summer night and was saddened to find the food was well below its usual standards. The owner came by and casually mentioned that the restaurant was closing that night for a weeklong summer break and that the kitchen was in the process of "cleaning out the fridge." Though that explained the subpar food, it did little to make me feel good about paying top dollar for aging ingredients, and it made me feel even less easy about recommending the place to my readers.

A few weeks after visiting another place I had extolled, a dish that was described on the menu as having morels came out with a less compelling combo of cremini and white mushrooms, with no mention of the substitution. When I asked about the switcheroo, the server looked at me like I hadn't a clue. "Morels aren't in season," she explained, as if I should have known better than to trust what was on the menu.

Hot food on a cold plate; details promised on the menu but forgotten in the kitchen, like gremolata on osso buco; bone-hard, undercooked beets in a salad; dry, overcooked salmon and a chef who—after asking me how I liked the dish and getting my honest opinion—shrugged and said, "Well, it's salmon. What do you expect?"

It's not like missteps never happened in France; they did, just not nearly as often. And I didn't demand perfection every single visit—I knew firsthand how easily things can go awry. I tried to be forgiving. But when the missteps piled up, I did have to wonder what was going on out there. At that private dining club I worked for, our food was consistent, night after night. And though the *Register*'s restaurant reviewer nailed us on a few things at the Meadowlark, we got our act together and got back to our usual high standards. For all the years I worked there, until the early-1980s recession, customers piled in because they knew they could count on us to get it right.

After a summer stint in France, it was hard not to notice how stingily staffed some of our city's smaller bistros were. Sometimes, only one or two servers would be on the floor to seat and serve customers and bus the tables; sometimes, they'd even double as bartender. One night, I rolled the dice on a terribly expensive wild boar entrée at a Mediterranean-focused spot; the meat arrived so tough I could not eat it. I looked around for our server (the only person who'd been on the floor that night), but the dining room remained bereft of staff during the time it took Dave to glumly finish his entrée while I tried my best to saw through mine.

When our server finally came back to clear the plates, I expressed my disappointment. "You should have said something earlier," she said.

After I pointed out she hadn't appeared since she dropped off our food, she shrugged and said, "Sorry," in a way that told me she was anything but. Why a restaurateur would put their front of the house in the hands of uncaring and inexpert staff was always beyond me, but it happened at a surprising number of places, most of which never lasted that long. I did not write about the tough wild boar and the indifferent service; it was once again the case where I knew the restaurant would eventually shutter without my help, and indeed, it closed not long afterward.

Certainly, there were a good number of well-staffed restaurants with expert, welcoming servers in town. I always made a point of giving them due accolades in print. I should also mention that many of the best servers were at places that weren't terribly high end. The bar-grills, the polished-casual spots, the pizzerias and pasta places often attracted a style of server who seemed to genuinely want to show you a good time. And those pile-it-on places that drove me crazy with their reckless portion sizes were often the places with the most good-natured servers.

Still, it was hard not to think about France when I encountered subpar service at our city's top-dollar places. Certainly, I didn't expect silverware codebreakers or gratis Armagnac tastings. I never expected staff to line up to shake my hand and thank me for my patronage. Such deep-seated hospitality is something you can always wish for, but you cannot outright demand it from anyone—not a friend, not a restaurateur, not a family member, not a server. It can only be given to you without your asking, and it must be met with gratitude and an acknowledgment of your good fortune.

Yet knowing that in my mind didn't keep me from feeling in my heart a sense of sadness when I encountered inexpertise and indifference. I wasn't sad for me—in most cases, this was part of a job I was getting paid to do, and it went with the territory. Rather I felt sad for the diners—those spending their hard-earned money on a top-dollar splurge. It was my job to steer them right, and I felt they deserved better.

And that, more than anything, was my France problem.

CONFESSIONS OF A RELUCTANT
WINE WRITER

Many (maybe even most) people I know have had misfires in their careers—stretches of time at lousy jobs. I do know some people, however, who always knew what they wanted to do, then went out and did it with aplomb. For example, back in the day, if you wanted to be a food editor in Des Moines, a great route was to go to Iowa State University and major in journalism and home economics. Some who did that became senior food editors at about the same age I was when I started copyediting cookbooks.

My approach to my career has been pretty much "go where the wind blows me," and oddly, it worked out—as long as I had the sense to blow back if I didn't like where I ended up.

One of the most fascinating places the wind blew me was into the realm of wine writing. Sometime in the early 2000s, a magazine editor called and asked if I'd do a story on a wine-tasting party, and I thought, *Why not? How hard can it be?* After all, with a little research, I can write about almost anything.

Of course, it was harder than it sounded—it took time for me figure out everything from what a varietal was to what malolactic fermentation could do for a wine. But after a while, I became one of the go-to writers for wine stories at Meredith. I think *not* knowing much about wine helped me write for an audience of those who were new to wine and curious to know just a little (but not too much more). I was able to pare down a complicated topic in easy-to-get ways that did what readers really wanted: make them feel more confident about choosing a wine they'd enjoy.

Then, I blinked, and I was writing a wine column for *Relish*, a national food magazine with a circulation of fifteen million readers. Suddenly I was getting blown (or at least flown) all over the world to write about wines at their source.

What luck! At least, for the most part. . . .

Many years ago, after my junior year of college, I studied French in an eight-week summer program at Université Laval in Quebec City, where I befriended a girl who'd made her way to the program from Northwestern University. Over the umpteenth Labatt 50 beer in the open air of an ancient stone-walled courtyard café lit by string bulbs in Quebec's Vieille Ville, on the last night we'd ever all be gathered around a table again, she confessed something to our little group of American students who'd grown close over the summer.

"I love you guys," Amy said. "I'll remember each of you for the rest of my life. But I gotta tell you something: I've hated learning French. Every minute of it, every noun, every verb, that ridiculous subjunctive tense, every one of those clever slang phrases our prof taught us like she was letting us in on some kind of inside joke. . . ."

"But she was!" I said. I told her that one of my favorite parts had been learning some slang—especially the swear words that came from Catholicism. They sounded mild to my Protestant-raised ears, but to the Catholic Quebecois, some were as foul as any sacrés (swear words) could get. When playing cards with Richard, my French-language conversation professor who became a good friend that summer, I loved it when he lost a hand, mostly because I'd get to hear him say under his breath, "Tabarnak! 'Ostie! Câlice!" Tabernacle! Host! Chalice!

I loved being in on the joke.

"Well, to me, learning French is like being pricked with tiny needles all over your body. Again and again," said Amy. "Every single time I walked into the classroom and sat down, it was like, prick, prick, prick all over again. It was a slow torture and I'm glad I'm done with it."

I hadn't thought of that conversation until I was being led over yet another slope in the soppy, snow-dusted mud of a vineyard while touring the Loire Valley on a press trip.

In the wine world, press trips are junkets put on by either wineries or winemaking associations, who invite writers, bloggers, and other influencers on all-expense-paid trips in the hopes of educating the media on their region or products. For a good stretch of years in the late 2000s and early 2010s, I wrote about wine for a variety of publications, including that one with fifteen million readers; eyeing the reach of my writing, PR reps would often invite me on these excursions. Through such trips, I've junketed through four different regions of France, a swath of Spain, Portugal's Douro Valley, a handful of major wine-growing regions of Chile, and the high plains of Argentina's Mendoza province. As a food writer, I also toured parts of Italy and France on such culinary-focused forays.

For the most part, being led through beautiful wine-growing regions and wined and dined by winemakers, trade associations, and marketing pros was a wonderful way to travel far and wide on someone else's dime. And yet, like anything seemingly glamorous from the outside, the trips had their strange and trying moments, from a walk through freezing vineyards in winter and the one-upmanship among trip attendees to the weird and well-timed presence of attractive young women peppered here and there on the junkets. While such moments were a small price to pay to see the world, I mention them here simply to show a more complete picture, including what lies outside the frame before a thoroughly Instagrammable experience is cropped and filtered in just the right ways.

I realize, of course, that there's plenty of room for outrage at a writer who has any complaints whatsoever about being flown across the world to learn about wine. But frankly, long stretches of the trip could be surprisingly dull. Imagine one of your favorite places in the world: the Rocky Mountains, the Aegean Sea, the impossibly lush Dordogne valley with its honey-hued medieval castles precariously perched on rocky outcroppings. Now, imagine being in that place for five days, but instead of seeing the mountains or the sea or those castles peeking out of all that lushness, you're sometimes stuck in a sterile, windowless seminar room listening to someone gas on about wine. Some stretches of time felt little different than any meeting you've ever had in an office with a whiteboard and a projector.

For true wine enthusiasts, learning about the minutiae of a wine-maker's craft is probably some kind of heaven. While I do adore wine, sitting in the seminar rooms I'd sometimes think of a quote gleaned by veteran food writer Betty Fussell when she interviewed a French farmer about his famed Bresse chickens: "'Like the wines of Burgundy, it is on the palate that one appreciates them,' said M. Poncet of his birds. 'The rest is words in the air.'"

Sure, I liked going out into the vineyards and learning a bit about how the grapes grew on the vines. I loved looking at the plains and the slopes of the vineyards, and I appreciated the poetry of words like "schist" and "chalk" and "gypsum," "granite" and "gravel," "marl," "slate," "pebble," and "shale."

And yes, I'd gamely march through the drill, respectfully taking copious notes while knowing my readers would never care about such minutiae. I always felt, especially in foreign countries, that I was an ambassador, both for the publication I was writing for and for the United States itself. So did, with very few exceptions, most of the fellow journalists on the trips.

Besides, for a short while it can be interesting to hear that schist (a type of soil) can add a kind of pleasant minerality to white wines in the Loire Valley. Or does it add a striking freshness? I've forgotten. But I do love the minerality and freshness in the wine, even if I can't always remember whether or not it's the schist that teases out these qualities.

I would have gotten more out of these trips (and gleaned more for my readers) had our days been spent making more true connections. Take me on a short walk through the vineyards on a sunny spring day; lead me through a brief tour of the barrel rooms and fermentation tanks if you must. Then, let's gather around a table somewhere pleasant where you can pour me a glass. Go ahead and tell me about the finer workings of the schist and maybe a little about the history and tradition and expertise that go into the glass. But not too much. I'm not trying to learn how to make wine; I just want to lead my readers to wines they might love. Yes, please tell me a story or two, but then let's just see where else the conversation goes. That's what wine does best, right?

Instead, that day in the Loire Valley went more like this: we were led on a not-too-brief tromp through winterish drizzle in the snow-covered vineyards, all of us shivering in our light overcoats as the wet melty snow seeped through our totally wrong footwear (the late-winter snowstorm had been a freak event no one anticipated when the trip organizers advised us on what to pack). The French winemaker, dressed in a heavy but chic wool cape and equally warm and chic snow boots that we all envied for their warmth more than their chicness, would not, could not stop talking about dirt.

"Oh, and over that hill, lies . . . well, follow me, and I'll show you."

Over the hill, more bare vines, more dirt, more snow, more drizzle, more cold wetness seeping through my shoes.

"But the slope, you see, brings . . ."

More dirt! I thought. But because we were all great guests, ambassadors of our nation and our métier, no one would ever have thought of even mildly suggesting that we were freezing our tails off.

After plodding through the snow-topped mud that seeped through my shoes and listening to the guide talking endlessly about dirt, I thought of Amy learning French in Quebec, and I could almost feel those tiny needles pricking into my skin.

The carrot at the end of these days was, of course, the beautiful meals at night—the rarefied creations of Michelin-starred restaurants like La Broche in Madrid, the humble-yet-sublime delights of Comté cheese fondue at a rustic mountain inn, a tapas buffet starring pata negra and sherry in the stone and wood-beamed room of a centuries-old winery in Spain.

The food and wine were always lovely, and what a privilege it was to be treated to such splendors. But now that I have fewer days ahead of me than behind me, nothing could drag me back to most of those tables. Always remember, it's later than you think; spend your remaining meals like the rare gold coins that they are.

On the first few trips, I'd revel in my great luck at being seated at such tables. In later years, however, the meals began to feel somewhat hollow. And most all were, without fail, overly long. For the first hour or so, dinner was a pleasure. The lift of the aperitif, the delights of eyeing the menu and anticipating what was to come, the welcome distraction of meeting the night's dinner guests, often a new face or two from local wineries or wine consortiums. And because I wholeheartedly believe in a dictum attributed to the former Duchess of Windsor Wallis Simpson, "If you accept a dinner invitation, you have a moral obligation to be amusing," I did my best. If I couldn't always be amusing, at least I tried to keep conversations going. Until, that is, about hour four, when I'd often hit a wall. Then I'd start banging my head on the table and pleading with everyone to *just stop talking about dirt*—in my own mind, anyway.

So, yes, imagine yourself in front of the some of the most beautiful food in the world, but imagine that what's missing is your favorite people. Instead of profound conversations or ribald belly laughs or at least the kind of unguarded talk you usually have over great food with those you cherish, the meals stretch out for hours as you sit, trying to stay "on" and act captivated by talk of racking and fining and stabilization and dirt. . . .

And then, just as everyone's almost ready to call it a night, some joker on the trip—a blogger who has to let everyone know he's been following along and he actually does know something about wine, asks a question about, say, cross-flow filtration. And suddenly you're in it for another hour. It's midnight, and breakfast is at 6:30 because you have to drive two hours the next morning to tour the next winemaker's operation, followed by four more that day, with each keeping you longer than scheduled because they cannot stop talking about racking and fining and stabilization.

Yet while the days were spent marching through barrel rooms and vineyards, followed by century-long dinners of great food but conversations either focused solely on wine or simply guarded and less than forthcoming, at the end of every day, there was some kind of magic to be had.

In those moments of dreamy exhaustion, just before falling asleep, weary after the long day's trudge but with some residue of the dinner's wine bringing peace and a sense of well-being to the late hour, I'd close my eyes and fall into a vivid dreamscape of the best parts of the day. Ancient vines planted in circular patterns climbing up the steep hills of the riverbanks of Portugal's Douro Valley. Chilean vineyards on an irrigated desert plain, so lush and flat, but with the immense Andes towering in the distance to remind you of where all that lushening water comes from. A break in a vineyard tour in Argentina, under a breezy white canopy with a midmorning snack of milky coffee and fry bread slathered in caramel. Autumn in Bordeaux, a bright spree of red and yellow vines—colors intensified against the muddy brown Gironde estuary and the somber grays of the chateaus. The mountain meadows of Franche-Comté in spring, buzzing and chirping with insects and songbirds and smelling of wildflowers and sweet grasses. A final dinner at a charmingly humble restaurant in the elegant city of Parma, spent tipsy and clowning with some good-natured Italian cheesemakers, all of us speaking in French for no other reason than because we all spoke it passably.

But I'd trade all the great-but-brief moments of every single trip for just one more day in Chile. While the food and the scenery were as stunning as anywhere I'd ever been, what I loved most about Chile was not Instagrammable; rather, it was a profound sense of welcome and a true desire to connect—which was given to me everywhere I visited—that I shall always remember the most.

When I arrived in Chile in May of 2009, it was late spring in the U.S., which meant it was late fall in South America. A handler was waiting at the arrivals area for Dave and me with a gift of casual fleece jackets, one for each of us. This was the only press trip where Dave had been invited along; in fact, the trip was organized just for the two of us.

"In case you forgot it's almost winter down here," the young man said, handing us the two handsome jackets with discreet and tasteful Wines of Chile logos on them. Of course, we'd packed for colder weather, but I was truly touched by this thoughtful gesture.

He took us to the hotel, where we were immediately offered the complimentary breakfast buffet even though we had not spent the night (fresh fruit, dense breakfast rolls with a pot of caramel to slather over them, and sunny scrambled eggs—cooked a luscious midmost between liquid and solid—especially hitting the spot). We were given a few hours to freshen up, but one of the great things about traveling to South America from most of the U.S. is that there's no jet lag. After an overnight trip, you'll wake up a world away and in a different season, but the time zone is either the same as the one you left or not too far off.

Our first excursion was scheduled at a major Chilean winery about two hours away from Santiago. *Here we go*, I thought, steeling myself for the long afternoon trek viewing the crushers and de-stemmers and barrel rooms and bottling lines and such.

But then, our guide told us, "Your host from the winery felt that, since you only just arrived this morning, you'd rather not spend a lot of time driving out and back from the winery. He's invited you to lunch in the city instead."

What? No trip to the winery? No barrel rooms? No bottling lines? I was heartbroken. Qué no.

Lunch was sheer pleasure. We went to a Peruvian restaurant ("The best food in Chile is Peruvian," said my host). We tasted through some great wines served with beautiful, bright ceviche; lemony-sauced, chili-pepper-sparked conger eel; and voluptuous caramel desserts ("We love caramel. Go to the supermarket! Check it out! We have entire aisles dedicated to it," said my host). He kept complaining about Argentine winemakers, but in a jokey, lighthearted way. (Chileans and Argentines have had their disputes, and not always in jokey, lighthearted ways.)

"Gah! Argentines! They drive me crazy! They're so glamorous and so good at PR. We suck at it!" he said.

I learned more about Chile and Chileans in that pleasant little lunch than I had learned a lifetime leading up to it. Sure, a winery's ambassador is chosen for the very reason that they are charming and loveable. Dave and I even joked later that our host maybe wasn't even motivated by our comfort and desires at all; perhaps he had a lover in town and this was his way of stealing time away from the winery. Whatever his motives, our thoughtful, self-effacing, Peruvian-food-loving, caramel-adoring, barrel-room-eluding guide touched us to the core.

Everywhere we went, the Chileans seemed to open up to us, going off script in ways that enchanted us at every turn.

"We don't love to admit this," said a winemaker over dinner in the Colchagua region. "But sometimes our alcohol percentages climb so high that we have to add a little 'Chateau d'Andes' to the wine."

"Chateau d'Andes?" I asked.

"Water," he said. "We cut the wine with water." He gestured out the window of the hacienda toward the far-off mountain range, its snowcapped, water-bearing peaks barely lit by the last of the setting sun behind us.

Another host openly and laughingly suggested that the real reason Chilean winemakers started trumpeting Carménère over Merlot was because of the movie *Sideways*. (In it, Paul Giamatti's character snaps, "I'm not drinking any [expletive] Merlot.")

Once Americans decided Merlot wasn't cool, export sales of Merlot plummeted, she said.

"Only then did Chilean winemakers start trumpeting what some had known for over a decade: many vines we'd been calling Merlot were actually Carménère."

Suddenly, she explained, Carménère became a "new" discovery, a kind of signature grape of Chilean wines. New discovery? Qué no. Marketing? Sí.

What I loved most about my visits to Chile's wineries was that the tour of the vineyards and winemaking operations was always a brief walk-through. They'd done their homework on me; they saw that I mostly wrote short columns for lifestyle publications, and my readers wouldn't care about much more than discovering a new wine they might like that would go nicely with the ambiance and food of the season.

So they'd steer me to a tasting room—always with windows looking out over the vineyards and the Andes beyond—and simply lead me through a delightful tasting of wines, always with honest, thoughtful conversations amongst the sips. They were as curious about my life in the Midwest as I was about their lives in Chile, and for brief but meaningful moments, wine did what wine does best, and we connected.

A few days later, at the Cono Sur winery, I spotted three flags flying outside the welcome center. The Chilean one rose above two others, the winery's flag on one side and the American flag on the other.

"Do you have an American owner?" I asked my host.

"No," she answered kindly but quizzically. "Why do you ask?"

I nodded toward the American flag. "You're flying the U.S. flag."

She looked at it and then smiled at me like I was missing something obvious.

"But Wini," she said, "it's for you. We're flying your country's flag for you."

About nine months later, I was tromping through the sloshy snow-covered mud of the vineyards of the Loire Valley, missing Chile's warmth in so many ways.

And then there were the pleasant young handlers.

After a few trips, I began to notice something. If there were middle-aged or older men on the trip, often at least one of our handlers was a decidedly gorgeous, young woman who traveled with us or at least appeared at dinners and during the more entertaining parts of the trip. Sometimes she was an American employee of the PR firm who organized the trip. Back in the U.S., she was probably a kind of assistant who made airline reservations, sent out wine shipments to the press, and Googled people like me.

Other times, these young women were employees of the winery or wine consortium; when not on the press trips, they might be given such tasks as hosting tastings at glamorous food and wine events and trade tastings, presenting product to wholesale or retail wine buyers and staff members of high-end restaurants (and mediumish-end restaurant conglomerates), and dining with wine press and assorted influencers who might be visiting their region.

What, exactly, did these women do on our trips? They might have tended to some mundane needs, calling ahead if—I mean *when*—we were going to be late to a winery, helping us check in to our hotels, passing and collecting glasses at tastings, and so on. However, I suspect they were mostly there to be a beautiful and charming counterpoint of the less compelling aspects of the day. In my most cynical moments, I also suspect that, to the unguarded, their presence at tastings could make mediocre wines taste a little better. At the end of the day's long march, some men would practically trip all over each other in their attempts to get seated next to these women at dinner. Curiously, on trips where the press group was comprised solely of women, these young handlers would sometimes be conspicuously absent.

To the older women on the trip, these young women were always helpful and congenial and by no means haughty. Presumably they were chosen for their personalities as well as looks.

One evening, the conversation among the older men got a bit raunchy, as it can after an evening of copious wine-drinking. Somebody made a crack about Viagra.

"Viagra!" interjected one old man—picture him with thin, dyed hair and a face spider-veined from decades of being a wineau. "I'll tell you what works better than Viagra!"

We knew. But we were hoping he wouldn't actually say it.

"Young women!" he bellowed as he raised his glass to the lovely handler on the trip.

It was an insult to the older women at the table, a bitter notice to those of us who *maybe* had a few years of shelf life left, and thoroughly insulting to the young woman, who shrugged off the so-called compliment with the kind of class that made her great for this job while probably thinking to herself, *I wouldn't be tossing that Viagra anytime soon, mister.*

Though that was an especially offensive moment, generally the routine bemused rather than bothered me—maybe because even in my twenties and thirties, while I may have been easy enough on the eyes, I was never the kind of looker someone would pick to be an ambassador for anything. Beauty was never something I could trade on, so the ravages of time have been somewhat easier for me to bear. When I look back on these trips, some of them coming up on a good fifteen years ago, I realize that these ambassadors—the young women on the earliest of my trips—are the same age now (midforties) as I was at the time, and they are likely no longer ambassadors. That particular way of things does not gladden me in the least.

Fellow invitees on the trip could elevate the experience greatly. Or suck the joy right out of it.

I remember spotting a bottling line on my first press trip. I became somewhat mesmerized by the regimented fluidity, the precision and graceful mechanics of it all.

"Cool!" I said, mostly to myself.

A fellow journalist—the young up-and-comer on the trip who had an ever-growing number of social media followers—overheard me.

"You act like you've never seen a bottling line," Darren said, hauteur evident. This guy hadn't said three words to me since we'd been introduced a day or two before. Now he wanted to engage?

Clearly, I had given my newbie status away. Indeed, by the end of the trip, bottling lines were boring. After the third press trip, so were barrel rooms and hoppers, crushers, de-stemmers, and fermentation tanks. And so were unfun journalists like Darren.

Press trips definitely had a hierarchy. You soon found out who the most important people were. They're the few who knew they could simply not show up for the afternoon seminar in the windowless room. They got to tell long-winded stories at meals without being interrupted. They got the plumiest rooms; if there was a Spanish count at lunch (and once, there was), they were seated next to him.

Curiously, the top dog was usually pretty nice. It was the on-their-way-up Darrens who you'd learn to avoid. Fortunately, most trips were filled with amiable enough people; you might not become friends after the trip, but you enjoyed each other's company.

The very best trips were saved by the group's bon vivant, often a middle-aged or older guy who was as far in his wine-writing career as he would ever go. He had had nothing to prove to anyone, so had nothing to lose by turning the trip into as good a time as possible. He usually drank a little too much; his jokes edged toward ribald but were never mean. He always made more fun of himself than anyone else.

On my trip to the Douro, we were staying in a private manor house of a port kingpin, and each room was different. Likely due to my fifteen-million-subscriber readership, I was given one of the plumiest rooms in the manor: windows on two sides, a step-out balcony overlooking the steep river valley, a bathroom replete with both shower and separate bathtub, a sparkling bidet.

After dinner, our gracious host retired, placing yet another fine bottle of port on the table and letting us finish the evening on our own. This particularly good-natured group started comparing rooms, openly laughing at the obviousness of how the organizers chose who got what accommodations. We figured out that the writers with the highest visibility had balconies and bidets; the next tier, at least, had windows overlooking the Douro.

The conversation went on like this. On other trips, one-upping could've been the order of the night, and a cagey writer who had an also-ran room would have stayed pretty quiet. Instead, we all one-downed each other for a while, until finally Dennis, a blogger of middling importance who had not yet weighed in, said, "Wait a minute. You guys all have *windows*? You should see *my* space!" His was in a near-windowless room adjacent to the kitchen; it was about twice the size of a proverbial broom closet. If the finish line was to bring everyone into a moment of true, unguarded camaraderie, Dennis handily won the contest.

On the first day of every trip, while we were getting to know each other, I'd look hopefully for the Dennis of the group. If no such pleasure-seeker revealed himself, my heart would sink. I'd fear that the trip would be flaccid at best. Or worse, filled with joyless one-uppers and true status-trackers like Darren.

That's another thing that disappointed me with some of the worst trips: there we were, a handful of food- and wine-loving writers, in some of the most remarkable wine-growing regions in the world; we shared splendid meals, tasted striking wines, and toured stirring terrain together. You'd think the least we could do was be gracious to each other and have a few laughs when the time was right. That was mostly the case, except when it wasn't.

On the best of trips, we all acknowledged both our great fortune and the promise or at least the possibility of making true connections that might even last after the trip was over. But it rarely happened. The first few trips, I'd dutifully write down everyone's name and contact info; I'd collect cards and look forward to keeping in touch. On our last day, I'd insist on taking a photo of us all together (curious that few others ever did such a thing). But once home, no connections I made among the journalists and influencers went deeper than our following each other on social media. I have a box of business cards of wine writers and influencers I can barely remember meeting. I have a few group photos of me with my fellow travelers, but I, too, stopped taking them after the first few trips.

The final night of the worst trip ever—the one with an afternoon spent tromping through the cold, wet, and muddy Loire Valley vineyard—we were talking about Woody Allen's *Midnight in Paris*. I'd mentioned I'd enjoyed the dreamy sweetness of it all, particularly Owen Wilson's wide-eyed fascination with all he met and saw.

"Oh, it was such a facile film," quipped one particularly esteemed wine writer.

"Give Wini a break. She's from Iowa," said someone else. Everyone laughed.

"Ha ha. Iowa," said another New Yorker. "You know what New Yorkers call places like Iowa?"

(Wait for it.)

"Flyover country."

Everyone laughed. I smiled and sighed at the same time.

"What a riot!" I said as the laughter died down, as if I hadn't heard the flyover quip a thousand times. "And it's kind of a coincidence, too, because flyover country is what I call New York every year when I fly to France for the summer."

Nobody laughed.

As I drifted off to sleep later that night, I realized that not only did I not like the worst of these people, I didn't like who I might become if I spent too much time around them.

It would be fair to ask why I went on these trips at all, especially after a few years, when most had started to become tedious to me. I suppose it's because smelling the sea air in Cádiz revealed the lightly salty qualities in some dry sherries. Or because tasting a Comté cheese speaks of the mountain meadows of France's Jura. And, too, enjoying sliced prosciutto served simply in ribbons on a platter in Parma helped me uncomplicate the ham's pleasures in my writing—reader, you may cease feeling the need to dress it up or even cook much with it. I went for those fleeting but truly significant moments that informed and (I hope) elevated the few words of print I was allotted.

There was also the promise of free time, an hour here or there every few days of every trip that made the trudges that surrounded them mostly worthwhile. While all the written itineraries stated a certain amount of free time in the late afternoons, that stretch was usually greedily devoured by winemakers who went over their scheduled time, making us late for the next winemaker, who was by no means interested in getting us back on schedule, and so on throughout the day, until we had all of five minutes to dress for the four-hour dinner that night.

But every so often, free time actually did happen.

It happened in El Puerto de Santa María, across the bay from Cádiz in Spain. After a morning of touring a nearby sherry producer, we sat down to a long lunch of shrimp, clams, mussels, barnacles, and sea snails ordered by the pound in the café's adjacent market, then boiled and spread out on the simple outdoor table, served with lightly cool fino sherry. It was the most relaxed and casual lunch of the trip, and it was also the most enjoyable.

At 3:30 p.m., we had one long promising stretch of the afternoon and early evening free before dinner.

"We could go to the beach," said one of the travelers, an older bon vivant kind of guy I had enjoyed. "I hear there's a really nice one somewhere around here."

"It could even be one of those nude beaches," I ventured, having read about the nudist beaches in the area.

"I'm sure we could make it a nude beach if we wanted to," he laughed. (I loved that guy.) A few others chimed in that they were game to go to the beach, nude or not; they made plans to grab their suits and meet up.

Tempting as that was, I felt the need to break away from the group. As they walked back to the hotel together, I turned another way, heading toward the Río Guadalete. Finding the riverfront abandoned and the drab river not very interesting, I walked toward the Castillo de San Marcos. But once there, I realized how exhausted I was after five days of being "on"—of listening attentively, eagerly taking notes, keeping conversations going. Of eating and drinking too much and not sleeping enough. Of being a good guest.

Heading back to the hotel, I found myself walking along a narrow street where random weeds pushed through peeling plaster of the low homes, where the iron-barred windows and doors were shuttered against the brutal afternoon sun. Nothing moved except a lizard darting here and there. No breeze. No sound. Everything looked overexposed; even the sparse flowers in the window boxes appeared bleached amid the brightness.

As I got halfway down the street, a bony stray cat quickly slithered by as if on a mission, and the heat suddenly seized me. With the unforgiving sun directly overhead and not a speck of shade in sight, the light became so bright that I had to stop, lean against a house, and put my hand over my eyes to slow the mad darting of stars behind my eyelids. A motorbike sped by, its startling buzz bawling through the street, its fumes making me momentarily nauseous.

As I tried to take deep, slow breaths, I had to admonish myself. After five days of being handled from one winery and meal to the next, of having every moment calculated and finessed, I could not wait to be alone. And after five minutes of that, I'm ready to faint? *Get a grip.* If I sat down, who would pick me up? Or would someone think I was a drunk and come outside to shoo me off?

Suddenly disoriented, I wasn't even sure I had been heading in the right direction. The river had been my lodestar, and I couldn't remember if it was to my right or to my left. Still, I knew standing in the sun would do me no good, so I slowly and unsteadily ventured up the street in hopes of shade around the corner.

And there it was: shade. Not only that, but there was a café, with a scattering of scrappy plastic tables and chairs on either side of the door. Feeling immensely grateful and very lucky, I collapsed into one of the plastic chairs.

The boisterous chatter I had heard coming from inside the café suddenly quieted. I could see it was one of those unassuming joints that likely bustled at lunchtime, when it served simple food from its zinc counter, but catered to old men in the quiet afternoons. It was long, narrow, and dark, with a bar on one side, a slim row of worn plastic tables and chairs on the other, some kind of slot machine blinking and occasionally bing-bonging in the back. A handful of aging men stood in a cluster at the bar and looked out at me.

Still feeling a bit unhinged, I began to wonder: *Do I need to go inside to order? Do I know the words to order what I want? Do I even know what I want?* There's always something unnerving about not knowing the drill in a foreign country.

About two seconds later, the barman appeared with a tall glass of cool, iceless tap water on a little brown tray. In Spain, as in most European countries, water is not automatically presented to the guest in cafés. But the barman knew about the sun, the heat, and maybe even the distress of the flushed woman at his table. I needed the water desperately.

"Señora," he said, patiently waiting for me to tell him what I wanted. "Por favor . . . quiero . . . quiero. . . ." Suddenly, only one thing made any sense at all. "Una cerveza."

Wine wasn't going to quench my thirst. Water was not going to chase away those last remnants of disquiet I had felt on the sun-beaten street. Coffee was out of the question.

I was grateful he didn't ask what kind or what size of beer I wanted. He probably sensed I could not, at that moment, think that hard. A few moments later, he appeared with his little brown tray. On it was a draft, a little larger than a half-pint, of a pale gold beer and a tiny oval dish of about eight green olives with a few toothpicks stuck in them.

I knew some kind of simple light bite was traditionally served with beer, but olives were the last thing I thought I wanted, having consumed half my weight in seafood just an hour earlier. But the beer was perfect. Likely a lager, it was cool and a little bit sparkly and just what I needed.

Is there any better kind of alcohol lift than the one that comes after a struggle? When the weight of some difficulty has passed, or at least abated: after a long day of tense meetings or an interminable trip on a congested autoroute, after narrowly escaping a pickpocket in the Paris Métro or nearly fainting on a dusty abandoned street in Spain, something purely magical happens after the first few sips of just-the-right drink settle in. As I drank my beer, I was overcome by a sense of well-being, of not only feeling good but of feeling in good hands. There I was, simply grateful and happy to be cared for in the shade.

Life began returning to the neighborhood. Nearby, a mother buzzed at a door and soon two young children bounced out. She walked down the street, each of her hands holding the tiny hand of an exuberant, chattering child. Other women wheeled small carts of food to and from a nearby supermarket. A shopkeeper up the street opened his rolling steel door, swiveling shelves of his wares from inside his cool shop out into the street.

I slowly savored my beer. Soon, I nibbled on an olive, then another, enjoying their appley, citrusy flavors. They really *are* fruit, I thought as I reveled in the daily life of this remarkable corner of the world.

After my stint in Quebec, I became great friends with Amy, the girl I had met there who thought learning French was like getting pricked all over her body with needles. We both happened to find ourselves living in New York in our twenties, and we tore through the city together until we both moved on just before hitting thirty. We lost touch for about a decade.

Then, nearly twenty-five years after we first met in Quebec, Amy and I had a nice long phone chat to catch up. I reminded Amy of how she thought learning French was like getting pricked with needles again and again. She had absolutely no recollection of saying such a thing, or even having hated learning French. Soon, we talked of things we did remember.

That little hippie-run café outside the walls of the old ville that made that crazy-good leek tart—remember how we'd drink a double shot of espresso there before going barhopping? Drinking cheap bottles of wine in outdoor cafés, staying in the old ville so late that we missed the last bus to Laval, and the cute boys from Vancouver who walked us all the way home. . . . Discovering Moroccan couscous for the first time in our lives. . . . Skipping classes for a picnic at those amazing falls with those guys from Edmonton. . . . Meeting each other.

In years to come, when I think of press trips, I imagine I'll be much like Amy. The Darrens and the cold, muddy vineyards and barrel rooms and bottling lines will fall away. I'll close my eyes and instead remember my lunch in Santiago with the Peruvian-food-loving host, the circular patterns of vineyards climbing up the steep hills of the Douro Valley, the red and yellow vines of the Bordeaux autumn, the caramel-slathered fry bread underneath a breezy canopy in Mendoza, a U.S. flag flying to welcome me to a winery in Chile, a Spanish barman bringing me the thing I needed the most: a cool glass of beer on a little brown tray.

IT ALL SPRANG FROM THE GOOD EARTH

Except for a few deliberate (and inexcusable) transgressions I've already described, I generally did whatever I could to make sure those I waited on went away happy, from not bringing out a sloppily plated entrée to steering people away from one of the few mediocre dishes on the menu at the Meadowlark (like our vile ratatouille crêpes). I absolutely loved being able to serve prime rib dinners (at below cost, even!), sought-after rarebit burgers, yearned-for sticky buns, and other truly good food to our guests. While I didn't adore working at the club, I never, ever wanted to see a member go away unhappy. I still remember a special shrimp dish that I recommended to a diner, and a pang of sadness when he told me he wished he'd stuck with his usual, the snapper en papillotte. Even though we comped his meal (which we always did when members were unhappy), I still regret misleading him, making his stretch of time at my table a disappointment. While he likely forgot about the meal long ago, I have not.

But where did that all come from? Why did I care so much about these strangers? Why do I still remember some of the people who sat at my tables more than forty years after I served them?

I am sure this everlasting care for those who sat at my tables, and later my loyalty to those who trusted me to tell them where to find good tables, started at the source of any good food. It sprang from the soil, the black earth that surrounded our family's farm.

When I think back to my days on my maternal family's farm in Greene County, Iowa, I so often relive a moment with my Aunt Patsy. *She leans over the wooden fence of the open-air pigpen, the nozzle of a garden hose in her hand as she showers the hogs to keep them cool on the hottest of hot summer nights. We're idling in the early evening, and I can smell it all: the sweetness of new hay in the hayloft, the muskiness of the hogs, the minerally scent of well water muddying the black soil in the pigpen as it drips off the animals. And yes, the barnyard scent of manure, which is present but never overwhelming—simply a natural part of life on a small family farm. Aunt Patsy hands me the hose and asks if I'd like to help. "They don't like this heat any more than we do," she says. I love standing there with her, caring for the animals as they grunt and crowd around the feeder underneath our cool spray.*

If I were given just five moments in my life where I could stop time for just a while, this would be one of them.

When I think of my grandfather and his garden, I am often reminded of the haiku by Issa that captures a farmer who, pulling radishes, uses a radish to point the way forward for a lost traveler. I've always been struck by the way the fresh-pulled radish, with its pointy root, is an extension of the farmer's hand. Whenever I come across this poem, I see my grandfather showing me a radish he's just pulled from the soil of his own garden, his hands as dirt-caked as the radish itself—he and the radish and the soil all interwoven, all one.

When it comes to wine and food, the French have a beautiful concept called "terroir." Literally, the term means "soil" or "land," but it refers to everything that bears on the origins of the foods we eat and drink. Vineyards, for example, can be impacted by everything from the climate, to the makeup of the soil, to the slant of the slope, to the proximity to the sea. The regional mountain grasses and other forage upon which the sheep graze will nurture the flavor of an Ossau-Iraty cheese from the Pyrenees. The distinct climate of the Modena and Reggio Emilia areas of Italy gives just the right concentration of acidity and sugar to the grapes that go into a traditional balsamic vinegar of Modena, and the generous sunshine and warm summers of southwestern France ripen the famed prunes of Agen to a delicate sweetness.

Beyond physicality, terroir also encompasses the history and culture and traditions—the people—who make food and wine what it is. I've often thought that the further we get away from a deep and persistent experience of terroir, the more our times at the table will be diminished.

Growing up in the 1960s and 1970s, many of us had at least some sense of terroir (even if no one would ever have known that word back then), even in Des Moines. Plenty of kids I knew had some kind of tie to a farm. For many of us, our parents were the first to move to the "big city." It was not uncommon to have grandparents still living on farms or in those small towns that sustained farmers and vice versa. Even kids who didn't have a direct tie to rural Iowa sometimes had some other kind of deep tie to the soil and food traditions. In recent decades, I've befriended descendants of Des Moines's southside Italian American immigrants. They often speak of the prodigious gardens their parents and grandparents tended in their backyards, often growing things beloved in the old country, like zucchini, cucuzza longa (a long, light-green summer squash that's shaped like a baseball bat), eggplant, and thin-skinned Ausilio peppers. Often, such families lived on their gardens during the Great Depression and throughout the scarcity of the war, and they steadfastly maintained them for decades afterward.

Even if you had no tie whatsoever to farms or urban gardens, we at least had school lessons about where our food came from. In grade school, they told us about this thing called crop rotation. Some of our earliest reading lessons sprang from books that featured farmers and the animals and produce they raised and grew. We were taught the names of different kinds of dairy cows, and we even visited a dairy.

More than fifty years later, I was talking to my lifelong friend Betsy about our first-grade field trip to that dairy. She remembered it exactly the way I did. We had gone to the Anderson Erickson dairy on the east side of town to learn how milk was processed. At the end of the tour, they handed our teacher, Mrs. Hibbs, a jar of cream. Of course, she knew exactly what to do with it. In our classroom that afternoon, she had us sit in a circle on the floor, passing the jar from child to child, each of us getting our turn to shake it and watch as this magical thing called butter appeared. Then she spread our freshly made butter on little saltines and had us each taste the sweetness of the butter on the salty cracker. To this day, Betsy and I both adore saltines spread with sweet butter.

When my mother graduated from high school at seventeen, her mother asked her what she planned to do next.

"I thought I'd just stay here on the farm," she said.

I can picture her saying this as she takes a break from the morning housework, lounging on the back porch, dressed in a stylish halter top and tailored shorts she sewed herself in the north bedroom upstairs. She's lazily reading a women's magazine. A light breeze lifts the leaves on the vines that nearly cover the screens on this June day.

"Here's what you'll do," my grandmother says. "You'll leave for a year. If, after a year, you want to come back, you can. And then you can stay on the farm as long as you like. Forever, if you want."

Later in that summer of 1938, my grandmother packs Mom's bag for her. At just seventeen, Mom doesn't want to leave, but together, they flag the Greyhound bus traveling west on the Lincoln Highway in front of the farm. Mother is slightly tearful but excited, too, as she boards the bus; waves goodbye to her mother, father, and "the little boys" (her younger brothers); and travels on to Omaha for secretarial college.

Except for a brief stint after the war, Mom would never live on the farm again.

Happily for all of us, however, she returned often, both before she got married and afterward with her own family—my father, older sister, and me—for weekends and vacations during the school year and long stretches during the summer. I always say I had the great luck of spending much of my childhood and youth on a working family farm but without having to do any of the truly hard work of being an actual farm kid. It was never my turn to get up in the freezing dark winter morning to milk the cow. I was never mocked at school for being a "pig farmer," as were my cousins, whose fathers, "the little boys," worked the farm with our grandfather—absent the family's oldest boy, lost in the war.

I might have weeded the garden; I might have had to fetch a pail of water from the well for my grandmother. Like most kids of my generation with any tie to an Iowa farm at all, I cut weeds out of rows and rows of soybeans. Mostly, I shelled peas, cut corn off the cob, peeled apples, and pitted cherries—all on that shady screen porch, in the company of my sister and cousins, as we joked, laughed, gossiped, and incessantly teased whoever was (quite randomly) up for teasing that day.

Yes, there were the usual tiffs and fits of childhood and adolescence. And of course, we all complained about the work. Still. To say that I knew where my food came from was an understatement. I've been terrorized by hens pecking at my little hands when gathering eggs from their nesting boxes (until I learned to do it with confidence). I've waited in the early evenings for my uncles and older cousins to milk the cow in the barn so I could watch them pour some of the warm milk into a broad iron pan and see the barn cats come running.

I have churned butter—or rather, I have shaken butter. My grandmother would put the cream in a jar and shake it until a ball of butter formed. She did this nearly every day.

And the animals. To this day, in whatever city I'm living, whenever I have a sink full of castoffs from prepping veggies—potato or carrot peels, corn husks, the tough outer leaves of a head of cabbage or lettuce—I can't even compost these handfuls of good, nourishing things without thinking back to the pigpen. Any trimmings of a vegetable that we did not eat went straight into a pail, then, after the dishes were done, straight into the pigpen. I loved watching the hogs in the waning light of the day, listening to their grunts and squeals pierce the quiet as they gathered and delighted in these colorful feedings.

Anything left over from any meat we ate—fat or gravy or bones—went into two old ham cans. Every single night after the dinner hour, the barn cats would be waiting outside the porch steps for these scraps, their feast.

But in truth, there wasn't much we didn't finish at the table. I don't recall ever being told to clean my plate; it was something we all did naturally. Recently, my cousin Debby (who grew up on the farm) recalled, "We never went hungry, but our mothers never put more on the table than they knew we would eat. They knew just how much work had gone into every morsel on every dish and platter. They knew exactly what it took to plant and harvest and freeze and cook a pint of sweet corn."

I remember when I was very small, I was running around a pathway through the outbuildings on the farm as I tried to catch up with my older cousins. As I rounded a curve, I came upon a flock of sheep for the first time in my life. The animals were being held in the pigpen, where I had, of course, expected to see pigs. I'd seen ponies, cattle, hogs, and chickens in the barnyard; deer and fox in the timber; great varieties of songbirds at the bird feeder; but never in my short life had I seen or even imagined anything like a sheep. Seeing these new-to-me creatures stopped me cold.

I forgot about my cousins, now way ahead of me and climbing the fence to a field that flanked the timber on their morning adventure. I stood and stared at the animals. They looked like dirty clouds with dark faces—as if clouds themselves had floated to the field, mingled with the soil in the farmyard, and come to life right there. They sat still in a huddle trying to blend into the mud and staring back at me, silent, peaceful, perhaps as in wonder of me as I was of them. To come upon a creature you've never even imagined before—suddenly the world feels immense, and somehow even then I must have sensed it was only the beginning.

And that was just one discovery on one day of many on the farm. Like the day my grandfather sat me down beside him on the porch and peeled back the husks of an ear of corn to show me the kernels and silks inside. With calloused hands and bent, arthritic fingers, he fished out one silk and held it up from the cob. "See?" he said. "For every kernel, there is exactly one thread of silk." I could hardly wait to run and tell everyone what I had learned.

Sometimes, driving through the highways of rural Iowa to visit my elderly aunts, my eyes sweep the vast landscape of vanished farms, each detectable only by a crumbling driveway and a copse of trees where a homestead once stood. Seeing mile after mile of row crops and hog lots, life on a family farm with just one hundred sixty acres of tillable ground and forty acres of timber seems no less than extraordinary. Yet back then, the long hours of our days and nights felt as natural and familiar as listening to the wind in the timber beyond the barnyard, as regular as hearing the clanging of a feed trap in the middle of the night.

So, what did we eat on the farm? We ate what the family grew and nurtured, what my mother, grandmother, and aunts canned and froze for the winter.

Dinner—the noon meal—was an ongoing rotation of beef pot roast, pork roast, pork chops, and chicken (the latter never any way but fried). Always potatoes (mashed or fried), always gravy, and whatever vegetable was plucked from the garden in summer or from the deep-freeze or cellar in winter. "Pasta" would have been a foreign word; instead, we had noodles, always homemade. Yes, noodles were always served with mashed potatoes as well. Why wouldn't they be? There's a long afternoon of hard physical work to be done.

We always had dessert, generally pies whose fillings marched to the beat of the season. First up in the year was spring's rhubarb ("pie plant," as my grandfather called it). Midsummer brought berries, cherries, blueberries, and peaches (bought by the lug in town), and then came the fall fillings: apples, pumpkin, mincemeat, and finally nuts—hickory and walnut—culled from the timber. Cakes were equally seasonal, with strawberry shortcake in June, peach cakes in midsummer, apple cakes in fall, and nut cakes in winter.

Supper—the evening meal—was often leftovers from the noon meal. As there'd be no gravy remaining, we'd likely have a creamed vegetable: creamed asparagus, creamed peas and new potatoes, creamed carrots. Sometimes dinner would be even more casual: a pot roast would be made into a ground-roast and pickle sandwich on toast. Homemade potato or cream of tomato soup (made from home-canned tomatoes) were specialties. If there was no dessert left over from lunch, Grandmother might open home-canned peaches and pass the cream to pour over them. Or we might have "sauce"—applesauce, rhubarb sauce, blackberry sauce—as sweet to me as any pudding.

Tomatoes and sweet corn both hit their peak in the same weeks, and that's when many suppers would be bacon, lettuce, and tomato sandwiches brought to the table piled high on one platter with steaming corn on the cob on another.

My grandmother was a legendary cook and proud of it. She would sometimes brag about how, when the Lincoln Highway was being paved in the 1930s, the workmen would pay her twenty-five cents for a meal at her table. Even as the crew moved farther and farther west, they'd drive back to her table for as many meals as they could, until the distance became too far to traverse for a midday break.

And yet, though the food was painstakingly grown, it was simply served. My grandmother knew better than to overcomplicate anything in the kitchen. Her main cookbook, which I have and cherish, was improvised from an upcycled textbook on ball bearings, with newspaper and magazine recipe clippings fastened to the pages with straight pins. While there are plenty of recipes for cakes and cookies, there are nearly no recipes for main dishes and vegetables. That's because my grandmother's recipes for these were always straightforward, seasoned with salt and pepper, then braised, roasted, or pan-fried. Vegetables were served equally effortlessly—butter, salt, and pepper.

While in the earliest days of the farm-to-table renaissance, chefs would often talk of how their strategy was to "source the best ingredients and not (expletive) with them too much," fresh, simple, local, seasonal eating was an everyday thing to those of us with any tie to a family farm. Years later, when working in restaurants that served hollandaise, it would occur to me that the sauce, while wonderful, was merely a way to compensate for the lack of flavor in the trucked-in broccoli and asparagus.

Did I mention we ate carp? Even by the time I was a child in the late 1960s, polluted runoff likely made it a bad idea to eat fish from Iowa's lakes and rivers, but we didn't think much about that then.

My grandparents loved to fish; the Raccoon River was just down the hill, and Grandma and Grandpa had a trailer parked at nearby Twin Lakes all summer for short getaways. We would bring carp home from the lake by the garbage-bag full, and what we couldn't eat went to the hogs—I can still see the carp bouncing around in the dust of the pigpen, still alive more than an hour after being caught. I can see my grandmother chopping off the heads of the flip-flopping fish, skinning and filleting them in seconds, then tossing the heads, tails, bones, and scales into the old ham tins for the barn cats waiting outside, who no doubt smelled the fish and came early for their suppers.

To me, carp was a treat—after all, it was dredged in cornmeal batter and fried in lard and served around a big oak table in the warm farmhouse dining room with full views of the gardens and fields that fed us, and around the table were those who had tended the farm and cooked what they wrought.

I remember the night of my grandmother's funeral (she died at 101). As I lay trying to sleep in the north room upstairs, hearing the hum of a machine in the distance, I looked outside and saw the lights from headlamps in the field across the road. It was my Uncle Bane, harvesting the last of the year's corn. He had spent the days after his mother's death helping arrange the funeral and spending time with family and friends, and now it was time to get back into the fields and harvest before the next day's rain. I don't know what it was about that moment—grief at my grandmother's passing, a sense that everything was changing and the world of our little family farm would soon pass as the estate was divided—but as I saw those headlights jiggling through the dark night, it struck me in a way it never had before: everything my grandparents, uncles, and aunts did, they did to put food on the table. Everything they did, they did for us. How could the table not have been a sacred place for me, even if no one back then would ever have said such a fanciful thing?

When we weren't staying at the farm, we were living sixty-five miles away in "the big city." We had moved to Des Moines from Cedar Rapids when I was six, settling into the brick house with the yellow door, a modest three-bedroom ranch just one house away from the freeway just then being dredged through town. My parents bought it on pretty much a fire sale from the Iowa DOT.

Like almost every family I knew in the 1960s and 1970s, we had dinner together every single night. Until my sister and I got after-school jobs, dinners together were an uninfringeable part of our lives. My father would walk through the door just after 5 p.m., he'd watch the news and read the evening paper, and at 6 p.m., we'd eat.

While my grandmother's cooking was mostly from scratch, my mother's was about sixty-forty. Although she crafted as beautiful a pie pastry as any good daughter of a midwestern farm wife, she did not eschew one-layer Jiffy cake mixes. While she never stooped to Hamburger Helper, she did not mind opening a can of condensed soup to make scalloped potatoes or beef stroganoff. Spice packs for chili and spaghetti, Rice-A-Roni now and then, and Dream Whip in the cupboard for a quick topper to dessert, if need be. She appreciated the way Velveeta melted in grilled cheese sandwiches and tuna casseroles.

But doesn't every generation love—at least a little—anything that turns away from the day-in and day-out stuff of their youth? My mother recalled that her mother always made mayonnaise from scratch. Sometime in the mid-1930s, at the farmhouse down the road, Mom's older cousins, Edna and Lyle, introduced her to a real treat: Miracle Whip.

"Miracle Whip sandwiches!" Mom enthused when she recounted the memory, the dressing being the thing she remembered over the meat of the sandwich, whether it was bologna, ground pot roast, or boiled eggs. "They just tasted so fancy to me."

Always, for my sister and me, the bread for the sandwiches in our school sack lunches was spread with Miracle Whip, and I'm sure Mom thought she was giving us the best there was. Years later, in the mid-1980s, when cooking out of *The Silver Palate* cookbook in my apartment in Brooklyn, I noted that some recipes called for Hellman's mayonnaise. Once I tasted it, Miracle Whip was dead to me.

Still, I do not judge my mother for sometimes using a mix or a can to speed up dinner. If I'd grown up wringing the necks of chickens with bare hands chapped from husking corn, sweeping Dust Bowl dirt from the floorboards three times a day, and helping the family scratch every bit of food they could from the grit of a small farm in the 1930s and 1940s, by the 1960s I would have looked at condensed soup as a beacon of salvation from the drudgery of all that work. I would have been first in line for an electric can opener.

There was also this: both my mother and father grew up on the edge of poor, as did most everyone during the Depression. But Mom often said, as many of her generation always did, "We never knew we were poor." Indeed, her father stayed afloat with a chicken incubation and egg operation he ran out of the farmhouse basement. He supplied eggs to nearly all the stores in nearby Jefferson. While photos of the era show the family in tattered clothes, they never went hungry.

Growing up in town, my father knew darned well the extent of his family's hardships. Now and then, they might up and move to a different house if they could save a few bucks' rent. As a boy, his mother, upon finding an unexpected nickel in some forgotten pocket of clothes, sent my father to the grocery store to spend it on five cents worth of cheese.

"Five cents!" the monger behind the counter bellowed, waving his cheese knife in the air. "For five cents, I'll let you smell my knife."

On his twelfth birthday, unbeknownst to his mother, Dad invited everyone in his class to his after-school party, not having the heart to exclude anyone. He recalls his mother slicing the cake as thinly as she could to make it go around; there were simply no means to dispatch someone uptown for more treats. One boy, feeling fleeced, demanded that my father give him his present back.

Perhaps because of this, my father never stinted when it came to food, and my mother followed suit. Their table was open and generous. When company came, there was always plenty in the serving bowls and platters she put on the table. When friends came to play after school, they were always invited to stay for dinner. "I'll just peel another tate-y," Mom would say, always ready to add another potato to the pot, another setting to the table.

Here's what's truly remarkable about all this: there was nothing at all uncommon about the way our family ate. Our meals were akin to those taking place in the homes of nearly every other kid I knew. It was as common to be invited to sit down to a meal at a friend's house as it was for my friends to be welcomed into our home. The food might have been different, but the ritual of the family meal was present and inviolable.

And when it wasn't, I sensed, even at a young age, that something was wrong. I once babysat a neighbor boy who was about eight years old to my twelve. His parents were going to some civic function for the evening, and his two older sisters were also out that night. So, his mother left him a TV dinner. I thought TV dinners were grand, and so did little Bobby. But what was strange was that they didn't leave a dinner for me. I heated up the Salisbury steak in its little metal tray, and while I sat there at the kitchen table with him as he ate, I felt overwhelming sadness. It wasn't that I didn't get fed—I knew my mother would have something I could eat when I went home. What made me so sad was that he was eating alone, and that it seemed natural for him to do so.

I always thought something was off about that home, and I was right. Many, many years later, one of his older sisters came back into town and we met for coffee. Anne spoke of her difficult childhood and youth, about how unaffectionate her parents were.

About her little brother, she said, "Whatever it was our parents didn't give my sister and me, Bobby got even less of." Bobby moved away when he was still quite young; he rarely came back to visit. He worked as a successful electrician, though he never married. Bobby's life had been a lonely one, Anne told me. He died of a long and difficult illness a few years ago. Fortunately (and miraculously), Anne had somehow inherited the caring gene and was able to be there for her brother in his final decline.

The table is not the only place where families show their love, caring, and affection. And a kind and generous table does not guarantee a happy family (though it can't hurt). But if you've been lucky enough to be raised where shared meals are a natural part of daily life for you and yours and just about everyone else you know, a meal served with indifference will always feel like a missed opportunity. Something will always feel wrong.

✒ 17 ✑

READER, I DID IT ALL FOR YOU

I resigned from the Datebook Diner role in 2012. I left the gig for many reasons. First and foremost, an editor at Harvard Common Press asked me to write a cookbook on the style of modern everyday French cooking that I had discovered during my summer trips to France. While I was able to write and test hundreds of recipes for *The Bonne Femme Cookbook* while also reviewing restaurants, I was not prepared for how much time it would take to publicize the book. I wrote my last review in spring of 2012 so I could do it all: book tours, cooking classes, interviews, TV appearances, library presentations, Alliance Française meetings, and going to any PEO, women's club, or group in a church basement who would invite me. It was a refreshing shift in focus to move away from the restaurant scene and into the realm of passionate home cooks.

Blogging about French food was a little less pleasurable. Blogging seems to be a necessary part of being an author today, but while I love to write about food, I absolutely loathe taking photos of food. For me, taking the time to do it right is like, well, prick-prick-pricking my skin with tiny needles. Nevertheless, if Harvard Common Press was going to roll the dice on a midwestern Francophile food writer, I owed it to them to do everything I could to move books.

I also wanted to source my food more intentionally and eat more healthfully. Certainly, there are some thoughtful chefs out there who are trying to use fresh, local, seasonable, and sustainable ingredients. However, there are not scores of such places to visit in any given year. Week after week of dining on indulgent restaurant food—even when I generally only ate half of what came on the plate—was taking its toll. My weight was creeping up, and my cholesterol was hideous.

Plus, I love to cook. I knew it was time to hang it up when I started to dread rather than relish dining out, when I found myself wishing that, instead of eating restaurant food, I could simply choose good ingredients and make them into something that's gratifyingly exactly what I want to eat. It certainly isn't fair to restaurateurs if one of their city's chief dining critics no longer enjoys sitting at a restaurant table.

Lastly, there was the ever-growing disaster of social media. My editors at the *Register* encouraged me to write a blog on their website, and at first, it was enjoyable and engaging. I liked the immediacy of writing something, hitting the "publish" button, and getting quick and candid responses from readers. Often, commenters took issue with something I wrote on the blog or in a review, and for a while, there was some thoughtful back and forth between my audience and me, with plenty of healthy disagreements that were usually respectfully written on all sides. At such times, I didn't mind being put in the hot seat. The critic gets criticized—that's only fair, right?

Then the trolls and cranks started popping up. For almost the entire time that I blogged for the *Register*, you could comment on my posts using a pseudonym. While I had to stake my reputation and put myself out there with every word I wrote, for a time, anyone could say anything in the comments section of my blog without revealing who they were. Often, it wasn't pretty. For example, when the topic of tipping came up, one reader wrote that the way he decided how much to tip was something his father taught him: "The bigger the butt, the bigger the cut." My days would have been a lot happier without getting regular glimpses inside the head of any random creep out there with a Wi-Fi connection. It only grew worse when I ventured out on Facebook and Twitter.

Sadly, once a few trolls popped up, some of the smarter, more thoughtful commentators peeled away. I once asked whether or not readers still enjoyed dressing up to dine out at high-end places. One commenter said she learned from her own mother that dressing well for dinner is a way to show respect for the restaurant. Some snark replied along the lines of, "I bet your mommy still dresses you." That woman never commented on my posts again.

While people enjoy watching online train wrecks, very few reasonable people want to be part of them. Soon, I was spending too much psychic energy on the trolls and habitual cranks, and that became dispiriting and time-consuming. (A word of advice: never try to reason with hostile online commenters who get to remain anonymous.)

Many comments were so head-scratchingly digressive, they didn't even hurt. Case in point: after I gave a five-star review to a local restaurant, someone mentioned somewhere on social media that they apparently spotted the chef-owner shopping at Costco. That led to a Facebook meme showing an employee in a Costco apron with a comment bubble saying, "Welcome to Costco. Wini loves our food." Somewhere else on the web, someone reported that I had recently flown home early from a trip to France to demand that the *Register* pull a glowing article, written by another writer, about a restaurant that I (supposedly) did not like. The *Register* killing an article because a freelance dining critic swooped in and asked them to? That's about as likely as me flying home early from France for anything but a true emergency.

I got pilloried for many alleged transgressions, from having a romantic crush on a chef to blogging while drunk. Most were so patently untrue that I could shrug them off. But what truly hurt was being called out as a hater, a snob, and the like anytime I wrote anything other than something glowing about a restaurant. It didn't shock me that chefs and restaurateurs didn't exactly love it when I wrote a less-than-glowing review, though in prior years, most had proceeded in a professional manner when they took issue with my work. It did surprise me, however, that (online, anyway), readers didn't understand that my role as a critic was not to simply gush about every meal but to help them decide where to spend their hard-earned money and hard-won leisure time, and that sometimes that meant doing the joyless work of telling people when I thought they deserved better. A chef once complained on Facebook that I didn't include him in a roundup of restaurants of a particular style. Never mind that his venue did not at all fit the theme of the article; he successfully rallied his people into a frenzy for excluding him. In response to my perceived slight, one of his minions posted a meme showing a woman holding up a sign that said, "Haters gonna hate!" Suddenly, I was a hater for not writing about a place, even though the place had nothing to do with the topic of an article.

And believe me, Facebook was no place to explain that everything I did, I did for my readers, that I wrote not out of hate but out of love—for the possibilities of great things that can happen at the table when people care. Perhaps the only place to tell that story is in a book.

Social media, of course, gives you a skewed version of reality; I suspect most readers continued to appreciate my honesty, but as one of my editors said to me at a low point in my blogging life, "Social media has made bullies or sycophants of us all." There are plenty of people out there who will skewer a restaurant experience (though often behind a pseudonym on a crowdsourced reviewing site) and an even larger number of people who will gush about great meals; however, the middle ground of reasonable criticism—which I unfailingly aimed for in print—fails to thrive on social media.

While social media was hardly the reason I resigned the gig, it was the thing I missed the least after I left.

After I quit reviewing restaurants for the *Des Moines Register* in 2012, an editor at *dsm*, a local lifestyle magazine, invited me to write restaurant reviews and food news for their four (and later six) issues per year. I was glad to take it on, as it meant never having to write a tepid review; I only covered venues that I felt thoroughly confident in recommending. It was also great fun to keep an eye on food trends in town. Best of all, no blogging was involved.

Writing four reviews in a given year rather than fifty-two made it possible to report mostly on restaurants that were going through what I considered hot streaks—a divine stretch in a restaurant's life span when everything gels, when the kitchen's execution matches the chef's ambition, when the front of the house finds its groove, and when food lovers start to catch on to the place, filling the dining room with an energetic buzz.

Finally, I stopped having to munch on the ubiquitous balsamic-dressed mesclun salads and enjoy finds like chef Lynn Pritchard's local greens and farro salad rimmed with chive oil at his astoundingly good restaurant, Table 128, where I also reveled in the likes of vaguely wild-tasting elk and guinea fowl wrought with precise and imaginative touches. Rather than reporting on that routine butternut squash soup popping up everywhere, I got to tell of chef Joe Tripp's version at Alba. The dish soared with unexpected touches—spiced pecan butter and squash-seed granola, plus a few dots of maple-syrup marshmallows—and yet, it never lost its focus, making me remember why we all fell in love with butternut squash soup in the first place.

At Proof, chef-owner Sean Wilson introduced us to Middle Eastern spices that were lesser-known around here at the time—sumac, za'atar, baharat, ras el hanout—and used them in dishes from rabbit terrine to marrow bone in ways that revealed just what spice can do for a dish without making the dish all about spice. A downtown hotspot called Centro has always been (and will likely always be) loved for its good nature, great vibe, and abundantly portioned dishes. But I loved it even more when I got to write about the more refined, contemporary Italian food that chefs George Formaro and Derek Eidson had started to also bring to the menu.

It was also incredibly gratifying to see midrange American dining move beyond its predictable pizza-pasta-burger routine. The polished-casual movement really took hold when a place called Eatery A opened, serving fresh and imaginative food (e.g., merguez, a spicy lamb sausage, served with polenta and a white bean ragu), served at Tuesday-night prices.

Perhaps the best thing that happened to the informal dining scene in recent years was craft beer. When casual diners cared more about what came to their pint glasses, they started to crave equally well-crafted food to go along with it. Serving thirty beers, cider, and mead on tap alongside food anchored by artisanal cheese, the Cheese Bar DSM emerged as a kingpin in the craft-beer, craft-food realm.

More joy was to be found further afield in Iowa when I covered restaurants for *ia magazine*, a sister spin-off of *dsm*. It was especially uplifting to see places tap into their unique sense of place. At Brazen Open Kitchen, chef Kevin Scharpf's bold yet fine-tuned cuisine fit seamlessly into the setting of Dubuque's formerly rough-and-tumble, now refined-rustic Millwork District. At Wilson's Orchard & Farm near Iowa City, chef Matt Steigerwald's hearty and convivial food is always inventive and precise, but never precious—he'll never let you forget you're dining in a rough-hewn structure made from the wood of two century-old barns amid a hardworking apple orchard. It all taps into a down-to-earth, good-natured vibe that I seek at this point in my life.

While the farm-to-table, locally grown ethos drives our very best chefs, somewhere in the 2010s, we got to a place where that wasn't the headline anymore. As Steigerwald told me when I interviewed him for a story, "I think any good restaurant today is sourcing as much as they can from five to ten miles away. Local is a given at this point."

What's the next great movement of our local and regional dining scene? Perhaps it could be restaurateurs who take farm to table a step further by moving the table closer to the farm (akin to Dan Barber's Blue Hill at Stone Barns restaurant in New York State, though hopefully without the stratospheric price tag for dinner). Ferme auberge (farm restaurants) in France are commonplace; could they become so here, too?

Wilson's Orchard & Farm has proved what a wonderful thing this can be. Better yet, they're expanding—they've recently planted an orchard outside of Cumming, Iowa, near Des Moines, and are building a new restaurant and market adjacent to the orchard. Soon they'll have company in the local table-to-farm movement. In recent summers, chef Aaron Holt gave a similar idea a trial run, staging occasional dinners in a beautifully restored 1850s barn set amid the gently sloped landscape of grasses, wildflowers, and timber at Lone

Oaks Farm in Madison County. Now he plans to take the concept to his family's ancestral farm, Doolittle Farm, in central Iowa, where his vision is to convert the 1905 farmhouse and 1916 barn into places where people will come together over food grown at and around the farm. As a farm kid once removed, I cannot wait.

Beyond my own anticipation, restaurants like these could help those who never experienced life on a family farm get a sense of what they missed, and perhaps a vision of something else that could one day be. Best of all, such a place could tap into the original intent of restaurants in the first place. The word "restaurant," of course, comes from the verb "restaurer"—to restore, as in to fix something that was broken. It could be a place to help restore our broken links to our rich rural history, to restore our spirit amid the beauty of a small working farm, and to further strengthen our connections to those who grow, cook, and serve our food, as well as with those with whom we share the table.

CHEAP WINE IN THE OPEN AIR

Why, then, with all this good news, did I decide to give up reviewing restaurants completely? In a job like this, you always know when it's time to move on. That moment hit me in the summer of 2019.

On a humid August Saturday, I was jostling my way through the weekly Des Moines Downtown Farmers' Market, a frenzied cross between an outdoor food hall and a crazy-crowded street fair. Bordered by the ornate Victorian courthouse and old brick warehouses-turned-entertainment venues, the scene was rife with smells of barbecue and kettle corn and a hazy blur of all the colors of the full-blown harvest in Iowa. I began making my way back to my car, arms heavy with two large tote bags of purchases, when an acquaintance with whom I share a love for Ireland stopped me near a sweet-corn stand and asked me about my recent trip.

Knowing this guy's passion for all things food and travel, I set down my bags, preparing myself for more than a few seconds of chitchat. When we started talking about Kinsale, he grilled me on where I ate. As I tried to recall the name of a place I had enjoyed, he broke in.

"You must have eaten at Bastion, right?" he said.

"Oh. I missed that one," I answered.

"Are you *kidding me*? You went to all the way to Kinsale and you didn't go to Bastion? It's got a Michelin star!" Gary went on to ply me with descriptions of the food, a play-by-play of each course, the way the chef gave him special treatment after a few visits.

I listened patiently, offering polite enthusiasm for his descriptions. Soon, his wife showed up by his side. He said to her, "Wini loves Kinsale as much as we do!"

"Oh! Did you eat at Bastion?" Kate asked. She, too, started to tell me about the meals they had. They asked me again what places I had eaten at in Kinsale, and when I told them (the one or two whose names I could remember, anyway), they nodded in a shruggy way that told me that of course my restaurants in no way measured up to theirs.

Soon the talk turned to Irish gins, and when I mentioned how much I loved Dingle Gin, Gary told me of more obscure, smaller-batch gins.

I would still be there now, listening to them regale me with tales of their restaurants and botanical gins, had I not mentioned that my parking meter was about to run out, giving me an excuse to beat a path away from them at last.

Soon after, I ran into a pastor I know who began to tell me about the food he'd eaten in Ecuador. He whipped out his phone and started showing me photos of his meals while I graciously affirmed their seeming amazingness. Yes, it all looked lovely—the seafood still glistened with the sea's sparkle. But after a few too many photos, I wanted to ask him: Do you get as tired of talking about Jesus as I get of talking about food?

Because these days, I'm more inclined to want to hear someone go on about Jesus than about the meals they ate on vacation. Jesus, at least, had a point.

Yes, Irish cuisine is astoundingly good; coastal waters, artisanal everything, long growing seasons, and talented chefs who find fresh new ways to tap into a true sense of place make it so. The botanical gins are exquisite—there's a wildness to them that reminds me of the blustery Irish countryside itself.

But had Gary and Kate ever started to wind down, I might have told them a different kind of story—about how we had blown out a tire on one of Ireland's insanely perilous one-lane roads, and how the first Irish people to drive by stopped to help, and how a woman across the way ran out of her house and beckoned us inside for a cup of tea and some biscuits while we waited for the wrecker to arrive. I would have told Gary and Kate how, when we finally arrived at our destination and told the Irishman who greeted us about the flat tire that had made us so late, the man had said, "Well, surely some nice Irish people stopped to help you, now didn't they?" Because surely, they did.

Alas, I'm afraid if I *had* told Gary and Kate the story, they'd have asked me the brand of the tea we drank and what kind of biscuits the Irish lady served.

That day at the farmers' market was just one of many times in my recent life where the topic immediately turned to food and *would not budge*.

You could say that hearing about everyone's favorite meals is an occupational hazard in my line of work. Naturally, people want to share food experiences with me, and for years, I welcomed the exuberance with which people told me of their finds. In the early years, there was a certain shared joy, because we were all thrilled and proud that our city, our region, had awakened from its meat-and-potatoes, red-sauced spaghetti slumber and been reborn into a scene that with each year became more ambitious, energetic, fresh, surprising, globally inspired, and locally purveyed.

Whether someone was giving me a lead on a hole-in-the-wall I might not have found or telling me that a new bakery-café I had written about had "turned her life around," I absolutely loved hearing about it all. And with Americans traveling widely—including a lucky 71 percent of us who have even traveled abroad—there's a world of culinary experiences to share. Like when a friend of mine came back from his first trip to France and said, "I get it! All I wanted to do was to go to the next quiet little corner bistro and have the duck confit!"

Indeed, had my conversation with Gary and Kate taken place in 2002, I probably would have relished it. But by 2019, I had hit a wall.

Besides, in my experience, somewhere along the way, sharing too often turned into a kind of showing off, less about making connections through mutual passions and more about one-upmanship. When that happens, food separates us more than it brings us together. When that happens, we forget what food does best.

During those kinds of moments, I often recalled the essay "Is America Falling Apart?" by the English writer Anthony Burgess. In it, he compares his current sojourn in Italy with his recent thirteen-month stay in New Jersey. In Italy, he says, "manifold consumption isn't important." Instead, what matters is "talk, family, cheap wine in the open air, and the wresting of minimal sweetness out of the long bitterness of living."

Clearly, it was time to let someone else write about the local food scene, preferably someone who would love hearing about everyone's favorite meals as much as I once did. Clearly, it was time for me to move on. I was ready to reclaim the pleasures of cheap wine in the open air.

The four years since that day at the farmers' market—which included long stretches of isolation during the pandemic—gave me a much-needed break from those conversations. I can't say I've missed the endless effusions about food and the photo-sharing sessions that I'd sometimes encounter. Yet I do miss having conversations about joyous experiences at the table.

These days, if you see me around, please do come up and tell me about the great meals you've had, but when you do, I would love it if, in addition to telling me what you ate, you'd tell another kind of story, too.

EPILOGUE:

THE GREATEST MEALS IN THE WORLD

Returning home from World War II, my father gets off the boat in New York City. Imagine this: crowds of New Yorkers are waiting for the GIs as they disembark, ready to treat them to a night out on the town. A stranger, the proverbial tough guy from Brooklyn with a girlfriend on each arm, invites my father and a buddy to a chophouse on the waterfront. My father never talked much about the war, but he could tell you everything about that first night home. The Brooklyn tough guy orders a round of the biggest T-bones my father has ever seen, and when the steaks arrive, this guy clowningly picks his up in both his hands and eats as if it were a sandwich. The girls laugh; patrons at the bar fight over who gets to send over the next round of drinks to my father and his buddy, still in uniform. I often imagine my twenty-six-year-old midwestern father, his first night on U.S. soil home from the war, reveling with strangers in a crowded chophouse in Brooklyn. And I think: *I doubt I've ever had such a meal in my life.*

But there have been moments—less epic but locked in my heart forever.

1977. My first French meal ever. I'm sixteen, in Paris for the first time on a high school French trip. On our first night there, our teacher, Monsieur Thelen, promises to lead us to a wonderful French restaurant —his favorite—but warns everyone that if we aren't downstairs by 6:00 p.m. for dinner, the group will leave without us. Slayed by jet lag, my friend Cindy and I don't awake until 6:15. Downstairs, the lobby is empty, and the desk clerk shrugs at our questions asked in bad high school French.

So we stumble outside into the streets of Paris—wide-eyed, sixteen, and alone—wondering around which corner we might find this wonderful restaurant that Monsieur Thelen had told us about. Once in the subway station, we stare at the map, as if it will say "You are here—the wonderful French restaurant Monsieur Thelen told you about is here."

I can still see him, this stranger with a headful of dark hair and a huge, bushy black beard who asks if we are lost. We try our best in French to explain that we're looking for this restaurant that's supposed to be really wonderful. We actually think he'll be able to say, "Ah, yes, that wonderful restaurant in Paris—I know it well."

Of course, he doesn't know where our particular wonderful restaurant is, but he takes my little notebook and writes out directions for another restaurant he thinks we'll enjoy: the Bouillon Chartier on the Rue Faubourg-Montmartre.

How could this man have known that this crowded, informal nineteenth-century brasserie would open our eyes to the otherworldliness of Paris yet make us feel at home, too? Somehow, he knew we'd be taken care of there. So we sit at butcher-papered communal tables under glass-blown lamps, watching the waiters in floor-length aprons bustling around with rows of plates stacked up their arms; we eat elbow to elbow alongside Parisians who can't understand our badly pronounced French, and whom we can't understand at all, but who share their wine with us anyway, playfully filling our glasses when we look away. This is the place where I experience my first cheese course—a four-franc wedge of Camembert served with that curiously crusty baguette bread. My love affair with cheese began in earnest.

Over forty years later, no visit to Paris is complete for me without a visit to the restaurant recommended to us, two lost American girls, by a kind and aware stranger in a metro station.

After the war, my father owned a restaurant on the square in Jefferson, Iowa, called Shoppe's Café. He got out of hash-slinging by the time I was born, but a few small details linger in my mind as if I had been there myself. One: He tells of how he used real vanilla extract for the ice cream he made, and how he nearly cried after a waitress once dropped a huge bottle of the pricey extract, shattering the day's profits on the floor. Two: An older cousin of mine still talks wistfully of the homemade apricot pie served there. Three: One day some hot shot came in and gave all the waitresses a five-dollar Christmas tip, except one girl—who was, my father thought, the one who needed it most. My father turned around and gave her a five from his cash register.

Homemade ice cream, real vanilla extract. Handing your waitress five bucks for nothing. "No wonder," my mother said, "he went out of business."

Yet in my mind's eye I continue to seek that restaurant in every small town I visit.

1998. We're driving to Tuscany from the French Riviera. We're making good time until we get caught in the traffic jam of a lifetime. Fumes thicken the air; it's hot; everyone in the car blames everyone else for taking this ill-chosen route as we move mere inches in two hours. Finally, we make it to San Gimignano at 9 p.m. on a Sunday. We haven't eaten, but we know we need to find a hotel. "Completo" is the answer—full—along with indifferent shrugs and turned backs at the first five hotels we try.

When we finally get a hotel, it's 10:30. The desk clerk says most restaurants will be closed, but she calls ahead and persuades a nearby restaurateur to stay open for us. We arrive, weary, grimy from hours in a car on a congested autoroute, still shaking from hunger, suffering from the lingering anxiety of wondering whether or not we'd have a bed, or a meal, that night. Looking at the menu, I realize the restaurant doesn't take credit cards; we've no Italian currency.

"We'll eat now and worry about it later," I whisper to Dave as we look at the menu. But the waitress senses what's going on.

"No money?" she asks.

We shift in our chairs; I begin a desperate pantomime that's supposed to mean something like: I'll go look for a cash machine. She smiles at this.

"Don't worry," she tells us—we, the sad and grimy, travel-weary strangers who are keeping her here too late tonight—"you can eat now and can come back and pay me tomorrow."

And so we eat, gratifying pasta, a simple bistecca, a few slices of cheeses; she refills our wineglasses, insists we take our time, offers dessert long after the last table has left.

1981. I've been working at the Younkers restaurants for almost five years—nearly one-quarter of my life. Home from college on winter break, I meet Paul, a new line cook in his early thirties. He is kind, and I can tell he's had some struggles in life.

The entire store, including the Meadowlark Room, has been rebuilt after the tragic fire of 1978. While it's a lovely, gracious, pastel-table-cloth restaurant, its one downside is that rather than offering a place where the staff can sit together and eat before a shift (as we did in the prefire restaurant), the cooks eat at a small table in the hallway leading from the kitchen to the employees' restrooms, while the servers eat in a pleasant banquette in the back corner of the dining room.

At Christmas, we're all offered a prime rib dinner, which we can eat during our meal break in the early afternoon. Noting that it's kind of sad we can't all enjoy a holiday gathering together, Paul says, "Wouldn't it be nice if, one night after work, we all sang Christmas carols together or something?"

I'm sure a few younger cooks and waitresses roll their eyes when our boss, Wilma, insists we stay a while after work to honor Paul's request. "It's the least you can do for a cook you work with all year," she says.

So, sitting over coffee and pie or whatever we feel like grabbing from the dessert cases, we arrange a few tables and chairs in a circle and sing some of the more well-known carols. At first, Paul seems a little sheepish, knowing that everyone is here because of him. A few coworkers jump up and scram the minute it's okay to do so, yet some of the older servers and cooks remain; the circle draws closer, making me want to sit a while longer, too. We come up with more songs we can all sing, joining in with what we know, soloing a few bars if we have to. Paul later thanks us and tells us how much it means to him to have someone to sing a few carols with; we thank him for coming up with the idea.

By the time I come back to the Meadowlark from college to resume my shifts in June, Paul has moved on, as line cooks so often do in the restaurant world. Though I never see him again, I remain grateful that he made us come together for a little stretch of time to sing Christmas carols in the empty dining room at the end of our workday.

1994. I've begun my career in food publishing as a copyeditor for little point-of-purchase cookbooks sold in wire racks at supermarket stands. I absolutely love reading recipes, and I'm enthralled by the knowledge and skill that go into developing, testing, and writing recipes that truly work. I never realized there was a distinct knack for such a thing.

And yet, I have an overwhelming sense of imposter syndrome: What do I know about editing cookbooks? I can't sleep at night for worry that I've let a mistake pass through on the page. Worse yet, sometimes my fears grow completely unbearable, irrational, and insistent: I am certain that some mistake I missed will change the meaning of an instruction . . . and cause someone to burn their house down or poison themselves and their family due to a food-safety issue. I can't shake these fears; they're with me everywhere I go. (I'm later diagnosed with obsessive-compulsive disorder, something I manage but still struggle with now and then.)

After Christmas, Dave and I go to Kansas City; we stay at a lovely old hotel downtown with its dead-quiet streets on a snowy winter weekend. The trip, with its forays to the Country Club Plaza and its gracious holiday lights, mostly distracts me from my obsessions. Nevertheless, I now and then think about one little copyediting mistake that might have slipped through on my watch—is crowd-pleasing one word or two? Hyphenated or not? Did I check that thoroughly?

Of course, it sounds silly, but for the obsessive-compulsive mind, it's insurmountable. During the trip, my mind keeps going back to it.

For dinner one night, we go to the Savoy Grill, established in 1903, with its Western pioneer murals, deep oak furnishings under high-beamed ceilings, and waiters in black vests with metal numbered badges on their lapels. I order lobster thermidor, and there's something comforting about this lavish classic (and a gin gimlet or two) that makes me forget my copyediting worries. But after dessert, my obsessions start to mildly sneak back.

We've struck up a few nice conversations with our waiter, a young man from somewhere in South America. He's a pro, through and through, with just the right amount of finesse, but no fussiness; he loves showing his guests from Iowa a good time. We're in great hands.

After dinner, as the restaurant begins to empty, we ask him about the other dining rooms in the restaurant.

"C'mon, let me show them to you," he says. He takes us back into the lesser-used rooms and even to the hotel's empty breakfast room with its stained-glass windows. At one point, he stops and shows us the vintage hexagon-tile floors laid by Italian immigrants.

"See that?" he says, pointing to an irregularity in the otherwise intricate-yet-perfect pattern of the tiles. "The craftsmen would always be sure to make one mistake in the pattern because, they said, 'Only God is perfect.'"

How on earth could this young man have known that is exactly what I need to hear at this moment? While my OCD will occasionally flare up in the years that follow, that night, I relax and think no more about any possible copyediting errors for the rest of my trip.

2016. It's been four years since I reviewed restaurants for the *Des Moines Register*. I still cover the food scene for *dsm magazine*, but my articles are less frequent, and I only cover things I love. It's a fine gig.

But for a special restaurant-week edition, the editor has asked me to do a little piece on a local restaurateur with whom (unbeknownst to my editor) I've had a shaky past thanks to some of the lower points in my social media life. I'm not looking forward to sitting down with him for an interview.

When I get to his restaurant, empty in the midafternoon, he leads me to a pleasant table by the window and asks if I want something to drink. Wine? Coffee? Sparkling water? I politely decline. He shakes his head and smiles, then goes back behind the bar, puts some ice in a glass, opens a quality bottle of sparkling water, and pours me a glass. He brings his coffee and my sparkling water to the table and we begin the interview. It's as if he can't countenance having someone sit at his table without something to eat or drink, and he certainly does not expect me to have my drink alone.

All is forgiven.

1977. Back to my high school trip to France. I am now staying a week with a family in their two-bedroom apartment in Montceau-les-Mines; the two teenage daughters sleep on the hide-a-bed in the living room so I can sleep in their bedroom. The family eats splendidly, three or four courses a night. And instead of glasses of milk, the teenage girls—and I—are served wine, cut with just a little water. *I like it here*, I think. In this industrial town where the father works in a crane manufacturing factory, deep in the heart of Burgundy, my love of France takes root.

Annie, the oldest of the two daughters, speaks English much better than I speak French, so when she's home, she translates for me. But she goes to school during the day, and I'm left with the parents, who speak no English. I quickly realize that while I know plenty of words, I don't know how to *pronounce* any of them. Hence, the conversations with the mother and father are awkward and laborious, with me often finally resorting to writing the words rather than speaking them. Nevertheless, they never grow weary of trying to communicate with me.

One day, the mother and father take me to a little café for lunch, where I order about the only thing I can understand for sure: steak frites. It will take me a few visits to France to learn not to compare the thin cut of meat to the big beefsteaks I'm used to in Iowa. But the fries, I understand immediately. Real French fries—with a crispness on the outside and a puffy richness on the inside I continue to marvel at with every visit.

I start to devour the fries with my fingers, but then I notice the French parents are eating them with their forks. When I pick up my fork and do the same, the mother notices and smiles.

"Pardon. Aux États-Unis, nous mangeons des frites avec les doigts," I say, explaining in thoroughly mispronounced French that Americans eat fries with their fingers.

"Mais allez-y! Faites comme vous le feriez chez vous," says the father, encouraging me to eat as I'm used to.

"Non," I say, and somehow I get out: "Quand en France, je fais comme les Français." When in France, I do as the French. It's a concept that the leaders of our trip drilled into us, and I'm so glad they did.

The father smiles and nods; he pours himself and me a touch more wine. And then he says something in words so basic, even I—with only a year and a half of high school French—can understand: "Notre porte est toujours ouverte pour vous." Our door is always open to you.

Our conversations suddenly become less awkward.

1995. At Wild Ginger in Seattle, I've just eaten the best five-spice duck I've had in my life, and I tell the waitress so. "Where are you from?" she asks.

I used to cringe when waitresses in world-class towns asked me this, afraid I'll immediately get the corn-behind-the-ears treatment. These days, I don't care anymore. But instead of saying something akin to the "flyover country" line, she asks us how we like Seattle, she recommends other restaurants, she encourages us to come back. She asks us if we want dessert. No, no thanks, we say. But she returns with a scoop each of ginger-coconut ice cream and mango sorbet, insisting we can't leave her city without trying them. Indeed, the spicy-fruity-nutty contrasts are unlike anything we've tasted, but the memory of those flavors pales next to the memory of her genuine eagerness to share something good from her city with a stranger from another.

1992. It is the last night of a trip to France; we splurge on a meal in a restaurant in Evian with views across Lake Geneva. The first course I order, oeufs en cocotte, is basically eggs lightly poached in a cream sauce and served in a ramekin. My stomach flops involuntarily as the barely cooked eggs stream off my spoon. Not wanting to make a fuss—it is, after all, our last night in France—I nibble a bit, trying to eat more cream than eggs. But the eagle-eyed maître d' immediately sees that I'm not enjoying my dish. "Tout va bien, madame?" he says, discretely asking if everything is all right.

Knowing how proud the French can be about their food, and how frustrated they get when Americans don't get it, I say in my proficient but American-accented French, "I understand that the eggs are probably meant to be lightly cooked, but—"

I need say no more as he gracefully whisks my plate away and later returns with a more well-cooked version. This I enjoy, not only because it tastes good (the eggs are cooked through, but the yolks are still jammy, all cradled in a rich cream sauce), but because I am simply moved—and will always be moved—by a restaurateur's commitment to placing in front of me a dish I will enjoy.

1977. On the last night of my stay with the French family in Montceau-les-Mines, the father takes us all to a lovely formal restaurant. I have my first coquilles St.-Jacques—scallops in a wine-laced cream sauce topped with cheese and broiled—and am surprised when that's just the second of many courses. It isn't until years later that I realize what a sacrifice it must have been for this worker in a crane factory to take us out to such a splendid restaurant, but there we were.

During the week, my French has gotten better; somehow I manage to communicate to the family that while my mother has never been to Europe, my father had been over during the war.

"Quand?" asks the father. When?

"Pendant la guerre," I say. During the war.

"La guerre?" he asks. "Quelle guerre?" What war.

"Deuxième," I say, putting up two fingers.

He shakes his head. "Vous êtes sûre?" he asks. Much younger than my father, but having daughters close to my age, the Frenchman thinks I must be too young to have a father who served during World War II.

"Quel âge a-t-il?" he presses, asking me how old my father is. I'm surprised at how insistent he is. Also, I don't know how old my dad is. What sixteen-year-old pays attention to that stuff?

He continues to press me; he seems to need to know.

I tell him I'm pretty sure he was born in 1919.

He sits back, does the math in his head. "Oui, oui, c'est ça. La seconde guerre mondiale," he says, acknowledging that yes, it was surely World War II; he nods as his voice trails off.

The next morning as I'm packing my bags to leave, the father hands me a bottle of champagne to take home with me. "Pour votre père," he says. For your father.

Unpacking at home, I give my parents some gifts I've brought back from France. When I get to the bottle of champagne, I say, "My French host really wanted you to have this."

My father, a teetotaler since the 1950s, simply smiles. It will take me a few more years and some history lessons before I understand this secret handshake between the two men.

When I look back at the meals I remember most and the tables I continue to seek, I am filled with gratitude to think of the beautiful things I've had the great luck to enjoy over the years: that inaugural, head-spinningly wondrous tom kha kai in Des Moines, fresh white asparagus in springtime Bordeaux, crispy-skinned suckling pig at Botín in Madrid, the most garlicky spaghetti with clams in Venice, soft and puffy fry bread slathered with caramel in Argentina. Crisp, minerally Rieslings in Alsace, thick, sweet Banyuls served as an aperitif in Collioure, unmistakably floral and feminine Borderies Cognacs in, of course, Cognac.

The descriptions of such pleasures could fill a book. While it is pure joy to recall the best bites and the best sips, for me all but a few of those memories have faded over time. What remains in my mind is what matters most when you sit down to each and every meal: the profound connection you feel with those who grew and cooked the food; the people with whom you break bread; and the people who are genuinely glad you're sitting at their table.

ACKNOWLEDGMENTS

Throughout my professional writing life, I have had the very best luck when it comes to editors. I'm grateful to every single one of them for continuing to hire me, assignment after assignment, year after year, which allowed me to make a living doing what I loved—writing about food and wine.

While it would be too much to mention every editor here, I must call out a few who played key roles in my work as a restaurant reviewer. Thank you, Kathy Berdan, for hiring me as the *Des Moines Register*'s Datebook Diner. Later, Doug Peterson and Kevin Cox became my editors at the paper. Lucky me! I remember thinking I'd do the gig for two to three years, max. But all three of you brought so much expertise and great fun to the job, I ended up staying for nearly fifteen.

Having Christine Riccelli as my editor at *dsm magazine* was another stroke of great luck. Is there any other editor out there in the world who would have let me quote Jacques Derrida in a restaurant review? I find it amazing how well we've clicked on most everything we've ever worked on together.

My good fortune has continued with the writing, revising, and editing of this book. I'm grateful for early readers of early chapters, including Christine Riccelli, Carol Roh Spaulding, Debra Monthei Manske, and Deb Wiley, who all offered insights that made the work better, as well as the encouragement I needed to carry on.

Thank you, Nina Mukerjee Furstenau, the FoodStory series editor for the University of Iowa Press, for saying yes to this project early on, and then for helping me shape it into the story I truly wanted to tell. I'm also grateful to James McCoy, director of the University of Iowa Press, whose sharp insights helped me add further clarity and refinement to this memoir. Many thanks as well to Alisha Jeddeloh for her expert and judicious copyediting of the manuscript.

And to my husband, David Wolf, my beloved dining companion for more than forty years (and my trusted first reader for more than twenty-five years). Who knew when we first shared that wonderful slice of new-to-us raspberry-almond cheesecake at Sheep's Head Café in Iowa City, that we'd be embarking on such great journeys (culinary and otherwise!) together. What great luck, indeed.

FoodStory
Nina Mukerjee Furstenau, series editor

Green Chili and Other Impostors
by Nina Mukerjee Furstenau

Khabaar: An Immigrant Journey of Food,
Memory, and Family
by Madhushree Ghosh

Love Is My Favorite Flavor: A Midwestern
Dining Critic Tells All
by Wini Moranville